Communication Tools for Working with Traumatized Children and Teens

also by this author

The Child's Own Story
Life Story Work with Traumatized Children
Richard Rose and Terry Philpot
Foreword by Mary Walsh
ISBN 978 1 84310 287 8
eISBN 978 1 84642 056 6

Life Story Therapy with Traumatized Children
A Model for Practice
Richard Rose
Foreword by Bruce D. Perry
ISBN 978 1 84905 272 6
eISBN 978 0 85700 574 8

Innovative Therapeutic Life Story Work
Developing Trauma-Informed Practice for Working
with Children, Adolescents and Young Adults
Edited by Richard Rose
Foreword by Deborah D. Gray
ISBN 978 1 78592 185 8
eISBN 978 1 78450 468 7

of related interest

**Conversation-Starters for Working with Children
and Adolescents After Trauma**
Simple Cognitive and Arts-Based Activities
Dawn D'Amico
ISBN 978 1 78775 144 6
eISBN 978 1 78775 145 3

The Adverse Childhood Experiences Card Deck
Tools to Open Conversations, Identify Support and
Promote Resilience with Adolescents and Adults
Dr Warren Larkin
Illustrated by Jon Dorsett
ISBN 978 1 83997 142 6

Communication Tools for Working with Traumatized Children and Teens

CREATIVE IDEAS AND INTERVENTIONS FOR RELATIONAL PRACTICE

RICHARD ROSE

Illustrated by Hazel Nicholls

Jessica Kingsley Publishers
London and Philadelphia

First published in Great Britain in 2025 by Jessica Kingsley Publishers
An imprint of John Murray Press

1

A CIP catalogue record for this title is available from the
British Library and the Library of Congress

ISBN 978 1 80501 290 0
eISBN 978 1 80501 291 7

Printed and bound by CPI Group (UK) Ltd, Croydon, CR0 4YY

Jessica Kingsley Publishers' policy is to use papers that are natural,
renewable and recyclable products and made from wood grown in
sustainable forests. The logging and manufacturing processes are expected
to conform to the environmental regulations of the country of origin.

Jessica Kingsley Publishers
Carmelite House
50 Victoria Embankment
London EC4Y 0DZ

www.jkp.com

John Murray Press
Part of Hodder & Stoughton Limited
An Hachette UK Company

The authorised representative in the EEA is Hachette Ireland,
8 Castlecourt Centre, Dublin 15, D15 XTP3, Ireland (email: info@hbgi.ie)

I would like to thank Paula, Ben and Callum, my heroes, and the TLSWi community across the world. I trust these tools will give guidance and confidence to all those who work with children and their families, who deserve our best.

My thanks also go to Hazel, and her mum, Angela. Hazel accepted my request for her to do illustrations for this book, and despite all the pressures of University, delivered. In the time that I have known Hazel, she has become an amazing, courageous, and successful young adult whom I am proud to know.

Contents

Introduction

At the beginning of any interaction with a child or young person, there is a need to explain what we, the therapists, are there for, how we may work together, and what we are aiming for.

I remember asking Dr Ricky Greenwald, a well-known clinical psychologist, to present at an organization I was working for, and in his talk he mentioned the notion of fairy tales in describing a therapy/therapeutic journey (Greenwald 2005, 2007). I took that idea, and from that I would like you to imagine, if you would, Sleeping Beauty awaiting her prince to save her – in this case her recovery to health is the desired outcome.

Nothing is easy, but then nothing that is important ever is. Once the prince has navigated the challenges, he gets to his princess and is able to revive her – not necessarily how we would go about it, but the importance of love and kindness is at the core of any meaningful relationship. As Dr Bruce Perry, a researcher, clinician and teacher, states, the greatest of all therapy is love (Perry and Szalavitz 2007).

In my world of thinking, feeling and doing, I have come to the conclusion that for this particular scenario to be successful and for the outcome to be met, the therapeutic worker is not the prince – we rarely fix anything. What we do, however, is provide the narrative, the language and the many signposts, the engagement, the care (the love) and above all, the commitment and the stickability! The prince is actually the child or young person who is coming to their own rescue...although there have been times where I have felt the pain of their journey. The princess is really the patient 'self', ready to be freed from the trauma that has immobilized her, while the prince is her journey of understanding and release.

The twist is that the princess and the prince are the same person!

To recover from her sleeping sickness, the princess must be patient (not that she actually has a choice...), and the prince needs to be creative and determined, and above all, committed to his princess's recovery. He must travel across miles of terrain, battle through painful thorn bushes, see his destination, and then, having survived all that, he must either slay or calm the dragon, depending on which version you read.

This book is my way of showing love to all those who are creative, determined and committed to supporting hurt children and young people impacted by early life trauma. I have worked in social care for 40 years this year (2024), with 27 years of life story work, and this book packs in all the approaches and tools I have learned along the way. It has been a long time in the writing, often in public libraries as I travel between training and conferencing (at the time of writing this I am in Singapore, but you can also add Canberra, Melbourne, London and Dubai, to mention just a few 'grabbed' moments!). I do hope that you will find the activities and case examples helpful, and as you assist your children, young people and families towards their recovery, I trust that, maybe in a small way, I assisted a little!

On a note of confidentiality and privacy, I have changed the names, gender, locality and wider details to protect those I might be thinking of as I write. The case work and details, including the illustrations, have been prepared specifically for this book, and are work-based, learned examples and not actual interventions. I have ensured that not one child or young person ever feels that I have betrayed their trust. If you do recognize some of the narrative, remember, you are not alone in experiencing trauma, and what you might see as 'your journey' is most likely not, as many have travelled where you have.

Setting the scene – this is me and this is you, but how do we get to understanding that this is 'we'?

It is helpful for those you work with that they have a beginning, a middle and an end to your overall work with them and for each intervention. Creating consistency, predictability and repetition within the engagement will support the notion that 'you might be of help, you might be able to hold me, and I might be able to let you'.

I see those I work with every two weeks, for one hour...this is not only manageable, but also sensible as it allows for the day-to-day of life to occur, and it means that you will be able to plan and commit to those you work with. If, like me, you also involve the parent/carer/support worker, then they can arrange availability with little challenge, and they can also process the information, activities and opportunities presented in the session you have facilitated.

If you can, provide the child or young person and those involved with an outline of your one-hour session, breaking it down into 10-minute time frames:

- 10 minutes: What's happened since the last time we met?
- 10 minutes: Thinking activity
- 10 minutes: Play a game
- 10 minutes: More thinking activity
- 10 minutes: Reflection activity
- 10 minutes: Calm and play.

You should find that as the sessions progress, the times relax, and more and more 'work' activity takes place. It is not unusual for the timetable to reflect the following after three or four sessions:

- 10 minutes: What's happened since the last time we met?
- 20 minutes: Activity
- 5 minutes: Reflection
- 20 minutes: Activity
- 5 minutes: Calm and play.

Overcoming reluctance

It is often the reality of our work that we partake in a dance of attachment (Gulden and Vick 2010) when we work with someone new. It is interesting for me as these are reflections of the other person's own internal working model engaging with ours. I recommend that you are observant in this dance as it can give you so many 'clue sets' as to the social, emotional, cognitive and physical competence of those involved.

This dance of attachment is often referred to as the 'Honeymoon period', when new placements for children and young people occur – the dance is between the child moving in with the new family and the family receiving the child. This 'storming and forming' as part of the new relationship, after 'forming', will involve all engaged to scope each other, as a hunter might in a jungle, although unlike the hunter being the only one looking, checking, probing and assessing, in this case, everyone is. This can be quick, slow or continuous, depending on what is available to assure the child or young person that the environment is safe. Many new placements for children fail because the new environment feels unsafe, unclear and full of potential unknowns.

If you just have in mind that the first time a child meets you (for ease, let's say that when I say 'child' I am also referring to the adolescent or service user/client from now on) they are curious about you. The second time they want to know what you want from them, and the third time, well, this is the time that they need to test you, to decide whether you are 'good enough'. This third session is a challenge for you – the child might be rude, attack you, refuse to speak with you or/and be very uncontained. Sadly, many therapists and intervention services experience this third meeting and state that the child isn't ready to do the work, and so the intervention is closed. In my experience, this was not the child's intention – the intention was to check, 'Can you cope? Can you keep me safe? I like you, but can you like me? Are you able to hold me safe?' So power through to the next sessions, 4, 5 and onwards, and they will thank you for this.

We need to capture the voice of the child in the work that we do. Therefore, we need to be able to engage the child so that we can get their perception and allow their story to be heard. Play is our first language. We may use pebbles, music, drama or any other media to gain an insight into the child or young person and their experiences. To engage in play, though, we need to find our own inner child. Play can be used as a 'relationship maker'...it's all about the conversations you share with the child. Play is engaging, play is non-threatening. Play is also the passport to attachment.

Let's take a moment to think about the elements of attachment (the way we survive) and attachment models (the way we get our needs met, our defence). Central to attachment thinking is attunement and bonding, and I would like to suggest two approaches that might support this in the relationship building between practitioner and child. The guru for attunement remains Daniel Stern (1983), a prominent American developmental psychiatrist and psychoanalyst, and I would recommend that you read up on some of his thinking, but the eight components or actions of attunement are the important context for me:

- Rocking
- Cooing
- Eye contact
- Holding
- Smiling
- Singing
- Talking
- Touching.

These eight actions require someone to action them and someone to respond. The parent and new-born baby will enter this attunement dance from conception to birth and forever more. Established as each second, minute, hour and day passes, they will know each other without the need for actions. Terry Levy and Michael Orlans (2014) state that a baby in their mother's womb will attune to the mother and attach to her throughout the nine months, and by the moment of birth, this relationship intensifies. Whatever happens after birth, that intense attunement, the forged attachment, will remain forever.

For those of us working with children who may not have continued this relationship with their birth mother, where the wonderful validation of 'you' has not been realized, where perhaps the certainty of attunement has been lost, our task is to remodel this. I often talk in conferences and training about 'clue sets'. All of us reading this book, we are all what we were, and how we have been shaped by the clue sets, the role modelling and the interactions of those we depend on will shine through. Whatever our parental figures did for and around us has set the pattern and clue sets to what we need to do. I recently read Robert Webb's autobiography *How Not to Be a Boy* (2017), and he candidly explains that he parented as he had learned from his own father's care of him – and his blueprint for his own early parenting did not work well.

The question therefore is, how do we re-learn attunement? That is, thankfully, easy to remedy! Although missing in many families, the simple approach is – play! Play permits us to engage, to be together, to laugh, to create, to achieve and to relate. Each of those eight elements of attunement can be found in play, and when thinking about rocking, singing and cooing, we all do this as we regulate in play – some might hum, some might tap or rock, and a few of us (sadly, for those I interact with) sing!

Many families have, to some extent, lost the art of play; many families I engage with do not play board games, word games like I Spy, guessing games and physical games. It is apparent in my interventions that the loss of play within the family or placement is a tragic loss of learning, of relationship building and developing trust, emotional congruence and safety. In the many years of my working life, I have regularly introduced games to families who have never sat down to play. Games like Snap, Memory, UNO!™, Snakes and Ladders, Connect 4 and Chess are all educational and emotional learning opportunities. If all else fails, games like Bugs in the Kitchen or fast games with immediate reaction, such as table football etc., these will all encourage eye contact and anticipation.

You will see that many of the activities in this book are based on opportunities for attachment and attunement through enjoyable play, fun, art and love – these provide the ingredients of recovery, new clue sets, attachment, trauma recovery and the healthy attunement of self with those who have authority over us and the wider world.

Attachment theory is heavily influenced by the early work of researchers such as John Bowlby and Mary Ainsworth. Sometimes we find at the beginning of relationship building that we talk of attachment and its fracture – children who have disorganized attachment and those with secure but unhealthy attachments, which, in the main, prevent the child establishing new relationships – early relationships children have with their caregivers play a critical role in healthy development.

Direct work activities

I have decided to detail each activity as a guide to working with children and teens in particular. These activities will sit alongside some case study material and some worked examples to illustrate how the activity was used, the impact and outcome. I have de-identified all the cases and so, although the names and gender may be altered, the fundamental story is accurate and true as far as I believe.

Please treat each activity as a standalone tool. Hopefully, by the end of this book you will have what Laurel Downey, a family therapist, told me I needed – an eclectic tool cupboard, with techniques for every eventuality, to use without hesitation when needed (Downey 2007, 2013).

Everything that I do I write on paper. I use wallpaper (or 1000 or 1200 grade lining paper) to record the ongoing discussions, working outs, questions, statements, anger and hope. This wallpaper is strong enough to hold paint, collage and colours, and once completed, the child or young person can see their hurt, their challenges, their joy and their more hopeful tomorrow.

With all these cases presented, I hope that these activities help to encourage the sharing of stories as they are worked through. This will then support the narrative towards a child's trauma recovery. In telling their story, we can bear witness and hold the child's pain while we share other stories of those involved in their journey. This provides the time and space to assist in reframing the narrative as a more informed and therapeutic story that has dealt with shame, guilt, confusion, anger and the unknown. All of us are a collection of stories that represent what we were to who we are. In understanding our story, we can move forward to a future not constrained or defined by an unresolved past. Stories are meaning, stories help us make sense, stories are something to lean on.

Key resources

You will need the following to do the activities in this book:

- Wallpaper or lining paper that is at least 1000 grade, and preferably 1200 grade (this has more durability), or poster paper
- Coloured texters
- Jenga® blocks x 2 sets
- Think Feel Do Bear or stencil
- Super glue such as Gorilla Glue® or Loctite®
- Paper glue such as Elmer's® School Glue or Pritt Stick
- Sticky pads, such as Post-it® notes or note pads
- You!
- Your young person
- Time
- Curiosity.

1

Serve and Return

UNDERSTANDING ATTACHMENT IN ACTION

For some time now I have introduced this activity to help discuss the impact of attachment and how, with survival and safety needs in mind, we shape our journey. This can be viewed on social media and my organization's website, but I feel that working through it yourself you can see how, by understanding attachment and its development, and when it is unhealthy, we can support recovery by encouraging children and families to weave a new carpet of attachment.

For this activity you will initially need two glasses, and later, a third. Fill two of the glasses with water to about half full (or half empty, depending on your perspective). Then get another glass and fill this to an inch (or a couple of centimetres) from the top.

With the first two glasses, identify one glass as the child and the other as the primary carer – in this activity, this is always the birth mother. Consider the child's water in the glass as their essence of self and that this is a child in the mother's womb. The mother's glass is representing her at this point expecting her child – imagine the water in her glass being her essence. With one glass in each hand, consider how each glass shares their essence as a reciprocal experience, and exchange water between each. As you do this, what we are showing is the interplay between the mother and her forming baby – so when the mother eats, her child eats, and when the mother sleeps, her baby settles. For a healthy womb journey, if the mother eats consistently, predictably and repetitively, then her baby will do likewise, and the glucose (the baby's development fuel) becomes a certainty. If the mother is healthy and emotionally settled, her heartbeat will be regular, consistent, predictable and repetitive.

As you keep exchanging the water between the two glasses, think about the heartbeat of the mother offering a 'beat' that promotes her baby to synchronize its own heartbeat with that of the mother's. This synchronizing beat develops the baby's unique rhythm of life. Rhythm is an important part of regulation, and so, as you exchange the water, let's think about sound, especially in the third trimester of pregnancy. Music is influential. For some readers of a certain age, you may remember as I do, Sony Walkman cassette players. As the famous advert states, 'Strap a Sony Walkman to your pregnant belly and play Mozart and your child will become a genius.'

To some extent the impact of playing heartbeat-regulated music provides a consistent, predictable and repetitive beat to synchronize with. There are several research projects that demonstrate that babies recognize music played in the womb, and that this calms them when in aroused states...indeed, some research has found that playing music at a heartbeat regulation for children who had 'lost their internal control' calmed them more effectively and efficiently than any adult might. Many practitioners, including me, play music quietly when working with difficult subjects, so that as we explore the hurts of the past, the heart doesn't follow the sad/challenging/scary stories as it is too busy synchronizing with the music.

The principles of EMDR (Eye Movement Desensitization and Reprocessing) are to provide a regulating visual or audible movement to distract the patient from the sympathetic nervous system's reaction to the retelling of their trauma – for example, many soldiers who have returned from distressing scenes of war, and all that follows, will struggle with the images and noises long after the initial experience. Metronomes that are set at 72 beats per minute will play out their beat through the night – as nightmares occur, the heart is distracted by the consistent, predictable and repetitive metronome beat, and not the horrors of the dream. For those of you who care for children who struggle at night time, with terrors and dreams, purchase a ticking clock and ensure that the tick is reasonably audible – 60 beats a minute will relax the heart and help soothe the child if and when their night terrors visit. And, of course, heartbeat-regulated music and bedtime stories told with heartbeat rhythms will also support a fretful child.

Let's get back to our glass activity. The water is being exchanged between the two glasses, and attunement and attachment is on show...then the baby is born and so no longer has the supply system they had when in the womb.

The baby has needs, needs that include food, comfort and sleep, and they can no longer have this 'on tap' – so they need to let their mother know that they have a need. Hold the child's glass alongside the mother's glass – the baby needs to *serve* to the mother – according to John Bowlby (1988) and Dr Allan Schore (2000), this is hardwired as a survival instinct, and so the baby cries. The cry is designed to irritate the mother in the belief that she will *return the serve* by meeting the needs of the child. Start to exchange the water again at this point, and consider that this *serve and return* is a natural discourse for the child and mother. Ideally this reciprocity will continue over the next 18 months. If the dance of attachment is consistent, predictable and repetitive, the child will know that they are 'lovable, worthwhile and able' (Bowlby 1988; Schore 2000). They will know that they are loved, protected and safe. In turn, the child's mother knows that she can protect, love and provide for her child, and this dance of attachment becomes secure and contained.

According to Schore (2000), babies are an extension of their mother for the first six months of life, and then they explore their world outside this zone. Mary Ainsworth suggests that the relation-ship and the preoccupation of a mother and child is established in the first nine months of life (Ainsworth *et al.* 1978; see also Bowlby 1958), and Arnold Gesell (1929) also suggests that children engage with the external world beyond their primary carer at nine months.

As you hold the two glasses, consider Peek a Boo – a stranger catches the eye of a young child of nine months or so. They both lock eyes in their mutual stare and then the child will often hide behind their carer. The stranger waits patiently, and then the child looks again; they lock stares again, and the child hides again. Using the two glasses, take the child's glass away and say, 'Unsafe', and then, next to the primary carer's glass, say, 'Safe'. Repeat this a few times to show that the child is investigating their world but relies on their carer to keep them safe. This Peek a Boo is an important attachment exercise, and with the two glasses you can show the final concept of attachment – if the carer can keep the child safe and allow safe exploration, then the child learns that they have a place in the world, and that the world is a safe place, one in which they belong.

The outcome of this positive experience is that the child has a positive internal working model, which provides a blueprint of expectation (Bowlby 1988):

I am lovable, worthwhile and able.
You are loving, caring and protective.
My world is safe, I have a place and I belong.

Sadly, many children we work with, and, of course, adults who have experienced difficult childhoods, may have had a different experience of their early life dance of attachment. Again, using the two glasses, let us visit this to help explain.

With your two glasses, let us restart the journey in the womb. If the mother is taking drugs, then so is her baby – exchange the water – and if the drugs are misused or harmful, and the mother continues to use them throughout her pregnancy, the child becomes as dependent on them as the mother. When the child is born, the drug supply is interrupted, and the time it takes to work through this absence can be very painful and disruptive. The drugs, though, are not the only issue; how does the drug use affect the mother's food consumption, sleep patterns, heartbeat and emotions before, during and after taking the drugs?

Continue to exchange the water in the two glasses, and then consider domestic violence. When a mother is afraid that she is going to be attacked, her sympathetic nervous system (fight/flight) or her parasympathetic nervous system (freeze) is activated, and all that happens to the mother will happen to the child in the womb. The mother's chemical production, or alarm state, is shared with her child and impacts on the baby's development.

Outside the womb, we have unpredictable noise as the violence is released; the baby in the womb may become startled by the loud noise, the explosion of emotions, and this will interrupt their development process and may mean that they await the next explosion or take time to relax and feel safe. Again, continue to exchange the water between the two glasses. You might wish to discuss other potential events that might impact, such as mental health, learning challenges and so on, but the impact on the baby in the womb is important to be aware of. The baby is born, and they need to relate to their primary carer for their needs to be met – so they cry to communicate their internal experiences of hunger, restlessness etc. Their expectation is that the mother (the primary carer) will return and gratify them, but what if the mother won't, or can't?

Put some of the child's water into the mother's glass, but do not return any water back. The baby will serve again, so put more of the child's water in the mother's glass. Explain that, as the crying doesn't work, eventually the baby will stop crying, and then place one of your hands over the top of the child's glass. You are demonstrating that the child has lost much of their essence and seeks to protect themself by containing what they have left.

If the child experiences this lack of return consistently, or worse still, they have inconsistent return and it is unpredictable, this may develop an internal working model that tells them that they are 'unworthy, unlovable and unable', and that their carer is 'unloving, uncaring and dangerous' (Bowlby 1988). As the child interacts with their wider world and the primary carer is not there to protect them, to communicate risk and to encourage engagement, the child might conclude that their internal working model of the world has no place for them, no space, and that they don't belong. Their Peek a Boo has not provided them with the surety to create a safe and unsafe perspective.

We are all about recovery, and so, using the child's glass and discarding the mother's glass, you should have a third nearly full glass of water, with your other hand acting as a lid. Introduce this third glass, which represents the carer, a new adult. This glass is full of essence, and you hold this next to the child's glass. Consider that the carer sees this hurt child and wants them to feel better, and mimic pouring the water from the carer's glass into the child's glass. Show that your hand is in the way and that the water will spill to the side of the glass and no liquid passes through the 'lid'. You can show that the child has not received any water. Do this again, and as you do, note that the carer's glass is starting to empty with no refill. Explain that, for this child, the carer may be dangerous, they may be uncaring, and the child has to resist the carer as they have no trust in them. The carer is getting frustrated that the child is not reciprocating, and those around the carer see that the carer is struggling and becoming strained, and they tell them. The carer cannot or will not listen as they cannot see the impact of this engagement. If this situation continues, at this point continue to show the carer's glass emptying as there is no reciprocal essence returning from the child's glass. The carer's essence in their glass diminishes and represents their crisis, and this may then lead them to believe that their own needs feel under attack. At this stage, as you are holding the carer's glass, they see themself as inadequate, the child they are caring for as undeserving, and if not attended to, eventually the child cannot stay in their care.

At this point, put the carer's glass down, hold the child's glass, and show that nothing has been lost, but also nothing gained. Twist your hand as if you are tightening the lid of the glass and say, 'I told you so, I told you I am not lovable, that adults are not safe' and then consider how this has been reinforced by the number of movements the child may have experienced in the past. The carer has experienced significant sadness, and may feel shame and guilt, but they never really stood a chance – love is essential, but it is not, in itself, a cure-all.

Let's go back to the carer, with the glass almost full and the child, whose glass is almost empty. We, as adults, are not designed to serve, we are designed to return – and when providing without request, often miss crucial opportunities. Instead of pouring any water, take the carer's glass and just make circles around the child's glass...and then think about actions that can take place around the child that may meet their needs – food, sleep, school, play, activities, engagement, friends and entertainment. Commentate on the importance of providing consistency, predictability and repetitive actions that show that what you say is visible, experienced and available. The child will start to see that things happen with or without their engagement, and that they don't have to worry about their safety.

A common experience for carers can be children who are placed with them, but the children don't trust them, and so care for themselves. Let's consider a child who hoards food in their bed, under their bed, or in secretive spaces. The child may have learned that food is unpredictable and that having their own supply will provide relief and a surety of safety. For the carer who is establishing that food is readily available and that the child would never go hungry, this hoarding may feel unnecessary, a memory of mistrust turning towards a reality of trust, but remember that this is one hypothesis. Until the child is able to work this out themself, the carer allows the hoarding that occurs, and may go further, supplying a Tupperware box or a similar container so that the child can keep their food safe and fresh, so they see the carer wants the best for them.

As the child begins to see that their world is becoming predictable, they may open their lid a little – this will be seen by a kind word, a hug or a simple thank you. Encourage the carers you are involved with not to react by pouring their essence into the opened lid; to just respond with an acknowledgement that this was noticed.

Once the lid is lifted, though, the child is vulnerable and may quickly become overwhelmed by the insecurity, and so they slam their lid back on – this is recovery! Explain that the act of closing their lid is protection, and that the child might shout, swear, break something, hit or self-harm to demonstrate that they are not safe and have to make themselves safe again. For carers, or for someone supporting a carer, explain that this is the process of recovery – one step forward, three steps back; two steps forward, one step back – and eventually the child will learn mastery of their protective lid. It will never go! Sometimes months or years later they may act as they used to. The trick is not to react negatively – be curious, go back to the glasses to model 'I will keep you safe'. If it helps, you are showing, as you move the lid up and down, that you are playing Peek a Boo.

This activity has proved so helpful for children and their carers in explaining the challenge of care and that, until the child is ready to attach, to attempt to attach they need clear actions that are signposted and reliable.

2

Bonding and Attachment

MAKING SENSE OF RELATIONSHIPS

In the work with children and young people, the concept of bonding is essential to work out, and this simple activity is a great way to explore bonding and attachment styles. This activity is to demonstrate the different types of bonds, which bonds are stronger than others, and what happens if a bond is interrupted. It is useful for the child who is having difficulty, for example, attaching to their caregiver (usually because the child feels as though they are betraying their biological parent or that their biological parent has betrayed them).

For this activity you will need:

- Super glue such as Gorilla Glue® or Loctite®
- Paper glue such as Elmer's® School Glue or Pritt Stick
- Sticky pads, such as Post-it® notes or note pads.

First sort out one large piece of paper and two smaller pieces, then, using super glue, put the glue onto one of the smaller pieces of paper and stick this onto the larger piece. With the second smaller piece of paper, put the paper glue onto it and then stick the paper onto the bigger paper so it sits alongside the super-glued paper. If it helps, write the type of glue used on each of the smaller pieces as a reminder of each type of bonding.

Leave the Post-it® note to one side for now – or, if you have room on the larger piece of paper, stick it there. Once the glue has had a chance to dry, remind the child that sometimes things do come apart, and that dependent on the bond, when relationships change, we have to understand that everything is subject to looking and being different.

Ask the child to separate the two papers stuck with super glue. This should prove almost impossible, and eventually the two papers will rip from the original paper and so remain stuck to each other. Look at the paper that has torn away, and explain that this is like secure attachment – whatever happens, the two are inseparable and are stuck fast. The bond is secure and cannot be removed – this demonstrates secure attachment – but remember that not all secure attachment means a safe attachment. Many children in care have a secure attachment to their birth parent, but the attachment might have been forged in fear, trauma or survival.

If a child has secure attachment to their carer of origin (birth family), it may not be possible for them to trust or attach to another mother or father figure – they already have this. The child will then avoid the attachment to a new carer and may become overwhelmed by them – to place these children in a 'family' may result in them not truly settling and attacking the family they now live with. Providing high-quality care without the presence of a substitute mum or dad, but with dedicated and trained care staff, can settle the child, and later work can take place to gently introduce them to a new placement or one that is less of a betrayal.

I am a supporter of good therapeutic residential care for children as young as four onwards, where the child needs high-quality care with a number of adults. For some children the intimacy of being parented by one or two people is too intense or causes betrayal and shame or rejection. With the replacement of a parent with another parent provider, the child may need to reject them, to protect their secure attachment with their birth parent, and so move from placement to placement, never able to settle. In residential care, work can be done to assist the child to make sense of their family and care status, and after three years, to then move to a family-based experience.

Back to our bonding explanation...

Now ask the child to try and peel the paper-glued pieces of paper apart – this should be easier, but it will still leave bits of the paper stuck to the paper it was attached to. It will also bring bits of paper from the paper it was stuck to. This is an opportunity to show' insecure attachment as we lose part of our self and gain parts of others. Imagine we have 7 glasses of water and each glass contains a different colour. Then treat each glass as a placement for a child. Imagine another glass, that if filled with water that has no colour added, treat this glass as the child.

The child is in their birth family and so they exchange their water with the water in the first of seven glasses – let us say that the first glass has yellow dye in the water. The child's glass is now slightly yellow and the parent's glass slightly paler yellow. The child is then removed from the family and move to the next placement – this second glass has purple-coloured water. The child and this placement exchange their water and now the child's water changes to a bluey-green tinge and the placement seems less purple. If we follow the child's glass through the next 5 placements, exchanging their water with the differing colours of glasses 3,4,5,6 and then 7 – what colour is their water by the time they get to the seventh placement? Crucially, what colours are now going to be exchanged with the carer who may have red only.

The seventh carer is not caring for the child only, but for the child and the previous additions of the placements experienced. The seventh carer is not caring for the child that began her journey with clear water, as the child has lost parts of who she was.

So, back to the paper illustration, the more that the paper is stuck down, separated and then stuck down again, the greater the loss of self and the insecurity that bonding cannot be secure.

But what of our Post-it® note? Well, this can be stuck anywhere, and does not require permanence; in fact, it may be so used to being moved around and potentially reused or thrown away that relationships don't matter and are not sought, many of the children I work with our 'Post-it® notes'. These children may annoy carers as they do not engage with them or the family – the family home often referred to as a 'bed and breakfast' – but to them, it is a sure-fire way of being safe, and doesn't allow for exposure, risk or heartbreak. The child does not attach because they are frightened that they will be moved to another family (do not attach to avoid the inevitable hurt and trauma they are forecasting when they are moved).

I remember a seven-year-old boy who had been moved from home to home – I was coming to see his foster carers, and as I was let into the home, he jumped down from the stool he was on, went to the coat rack and got his coat. He then came to me, held my hand and started to walk me to the door, ready for me to take him to the next family.

3

The Hands Activity

IT'S ALL IN THE HANDS! CREATING
STORY STEMS FROM SCRATCH

Most children and young people who have experienced trauma will automatically assume that you are just another person in their young lives who will leave them. This might sound harsh, but many young people in care have experienced multiple relationships with adults who are present and then gone – why would you be any different?

Social care is a profession. As we move and gain experience, as we learn and grow, the profession offers progression, and as with progression, loss is the result for those we interact with. The average 'work span' of a social worker in the role they occupy is about 11 months, long enough to be something to someone, long enough to make the relationship, and long enough to grieve for those who leave you.

It is my experience that children and young people who meet me for the first time are considering either 'how to please me', 'how to get rid of me' or 'how to cope with me'. They know that I am there for a reason, but what does that mean? It can't be good, it can't be that they want to know me, so it must be to do something to them: 'I know he is coming to see me, but what next???'

Dr Perry reminds us that the greatest and most powerful tool for trauma recovery is as simple as establishing a relationship with love. But how can we show love? Is this actually an appropriate recommendation for traumatized children? Kim Golding (2017) expands on Dan Hughes' (2004) concept of PACE as PLACE (Playfulness, Acceptance, Curiosity and Empathy) with Love. The concept of love implies a relationship that at times has to be unconditional – to show interest and accept the potential of disinterest! Those readers who have read my previous books will know that unconditional positive regard and love for each other is the quality underpinning any intervention.

This thinking led me to introduce the notion of the hand – the way that we first accept someone new by shaking the opposite person's right hand with our right hand, taking the calculated risk of friendship while keeping our shield in our left hand.

Relationship is key to recovery!

A few years ago, I was told about a survey which had been carried out in the North of England. This asked children about to leave care if they knew the name of their social worker. Most did, but most also replied that they knew nothing about the social worker's life, and yet their own story had been shared by all. Sharing lives and sharing stories is central to relational building, and in the process, while we learn about each other, we share commonalities, we build confidence, surety, self-worth and belonging. In other words, we need to share 'us', mindfully and openly, because stories are reciprocal, designed to be heard, shared, discussed and then passed on.

For this activity, try and use the wallpaper that has already been suggested (sheets of A3 paper are also fine). Then, invite everyone to place their writing hand palm down on the wallpaper and with a colour texter/pen, to draw around each other's hand (including yours) with their non-writing hand. This activity is fun, and provides touch, care and contribution, but make sure that everyone involved draws around a hand at the same time. At the end of this activity you should have a series of hand-shaped drawings. These will be small hands and big hands, with clear and not so clear fingers, fat fingers, thin fingers, maybe missing fingers – and fun.

Once the hands are drawn, ask the person to your left to write your name in the wrist area of your hand, in this case, R I C H A R D. By doing this, you are validating your name and those you are working with. In social work, children and young people are constantly having their names spelt differently in their files, and foster carers' names are formal in the files but often informal at home – for example Margaret may be known as Mags. This way we can identify who we are and our preferred name, so providing authenticity for all those taking part.

Once this is done, invite everyone to write (or write for them) in their four fingers an activity that they enjoy doing, and ensure you do the same thing! This leaves the thumbs. Ask everyone to write what they love to do in their thumb area, and ensure that you do the same with your own thumb. I often do this activity, and in doing so, I am providing five story stems that I am inviting discussions around, and seeing five story stems from each of those involved.

As an example, my hand will typically have written in each finger 'Audible', 'Driving', 'Family' and my dog, 'Marmite', and in my thumb I would have my 'PlayStation 5'! As the hands are completed, we can see each other's hands and identify what areas we have in common and so develop joint interest through sharing; we can also explore unique activities and find out more about them. My PlayStation 5 is my favourite thing as I can 'disappear' into the multiverse and leave, for a moment, the stress and worries of the reality of my life and the impact of hearing and thinking and talking about trauma. I argue (especially to my wife) that I *need* to play these games to keep connected with the children and young people I work with. I *need* to understand Minecraft™, Peppa Pig™ and SpongeBob Square Pants, let alone Fortnite™, Call of Duty® and Mario Kart™! Of course, this is not the driving factor – I just like playing the games, and sometimes I need to escape outside my current world.

This simple activity provides opportunities to explore a little more information about the person, and everyone else gets to share their information too. It sets the groundwork for future therapy and acts as a bit of a 'Get to know you' session. It creates a safe environment for sharing information. In short, it takes the pressure of what I want from 'you' to what we can share about 'us'. It used to be that professionals were told not to talk about their lives as the complex world of the child was a challenge that did not need to be added to. Thankfully, we have grown to realize that sharing lives and sharing stories is essential – not just for the relational opportunities it provides, but also for the setting, and sometimes resetting, of 'clue sets'.

Clue sets are what we are given as we grow from our entry into the world until our exit, often modelled by those who have authority over our very being. If we experience love, care, equality and respect, we replicate these experiences; they become not only an expectation but also a relational language. If we experience anger, hate, hurt and fear, we learn these and expect others to experience the same; this becomes our language.

One of my favourite books is *The Wizard of Oz* (Baum 1900). Towards the end of the book, the Tin Man asks for a heart, and the Wizard replies, 'a heart is not judged on how much you love but how much you are loved' – clue sets: 'I am worthy and I make a difference' is so important, and learning 'I am worthless and I am insignificant' is so heart breaking. This simple activity is effective and explores what I can do, what I am, and what I do!

Let's consider a 10-year-old boy – we'll call him Rishi. He has had a very sad start in life. In his mother's womb he suffered drug misuse and domestic violence; he was born addicted to heroin and left in the care of his birth mother and her partner for three years. He came to social services' view when he was admitted to the local hospital with broken ribs, a result of 'accidental harm' – caused as he got caught between his mother and her partner violently arguing. He had never met his aunt, but social services contacted her to see if she might care for him. She wanted to, but the parenting capacity assessment was not viable. When Rishi was four, in a settled placement with foster carers, he was then allowed to live with his aunt, which for him was a second loss. Sadly, within six months, his aunt fell ill and died. Rishi went back into the care of another family (his third loss). Five families later, he was fortunate to meet a carer who wanted to give him a forever family. He was adopted very quickly and by the age of seven he was the legal child of his adopted mother, Mischa.

This is a common case example in my work as a therapeutic life story worker, as Mischa had regrettably concluded that she could no longer cope with the demands and impact of caring for Rishi – she stated that he was overwhelming, that she felt suffocated by him, and that she could not engage with what she needed as he was all-encompassing of her.

In this worked example, my first visit would be to attempt the hands activity. Rishi wrote that he liked his mum, cuddles with mum, Newcastle Utd, goalkeeping and that he loved his Nintendo Switch™. His carer wrote (at the same time) that she liked reading, days out with Rishi, theatre, listening to classical music, and she loved to learn new things about the world.

Take a little time and think about what these hands are telling us, the interplay, relationship, status and personality – hypothesize what is happening here. Obviously, we can only surmise that it helps to listen. If you were facilitating this exercise, you would have your hand completed too – but the reality is that the families you work with will not really be interested in you. You might hypothesize that in this case Rishi is needing relationships to meet his needs – you cannot be a goalkeeper if there is no one to take a shot, and it is not much fun supporting a team if no one else does. You might go further and consider that Rishi's carer is more of an introvert, that she enjoys quiet and solitude to enable her time to read, to have silence to enjoy a film, and the space to learn new things.

Hypothesis is helpful – it allows us to test – and test we do. We are all a collection of stories; we communicate through narrative. As the facilitator of this activity, choose a finger on the child's hand – in our worked example I would say to Rishi, 'I see you have written "Goalkeeping" – tell me about that.' Rishi might reply that he is really good at goalkeeping, but 'rubbish' at all other sports, and that no one is as good a goalkeeper as him at school.

As Rishi tells his story, appreciating his way of navigating a space and a place, strategically identifying and acting on the opportunity to be part of, rather than apart, you can see how clever he is. Having explored one of Rishi's story stems, we can then explore one of his carers' story stems. For example, 'I see you like the theatre – tell me about that.' Mischa may respond with a look towards Rishi and then resignation, 'I haven't been to the theatre since he has been placed with me.'

With these responses, which I would write on the wallpaper, I can begin to assess both Rishi and Mischa's outlook on themselves and each other, and how this defines their relationship and its qualities and challenges. You might conclude, after Mischa portrayed her interests and how these were not being met, with an understanding of her loss of identity and her status, both as a person and as a carer. How caring for Rishi has been costly for her own needs, and that she feels unable to meet his needs.

Whereas with Rishi's story of belonging, or his need to belong, of his fear of being alone (as you can see in his history, he has already lost three main carers), you might comprehend his fear that he might lose Mischa. He keeps her in his view, dominating her space and being ever-present. If we can reflect on what we have, these 10 story stems, as they are told, provide 10 'opportunities' to make sense of Rishi, Mischa and their relationship. Done early, the hands activity provides substance to the potential interventions and assessments; it is fun, but also revealing.

As you progress with work with the child and those around them, you can change the focus of what gets written onto the fingers and thumb – as an example, four things (fingers) that are going well at school and one thing (thumb) that is not going well. You could complete a hand about relationships, contact, emotions and family. It is, indeed, all in the hands! Draw around your hand and see where your stories and the stories of others take you.

4

Footsteps Left Behind

Using footsteps gives a sense of movement, and so, using wallpaper or lining paper, you can invite the child you are working with to put their feet into poster paint (using a paint tray works well). I would suggest that you use washable paint and have a tarpaulin or old newspapers to protect the floor. As the child walks along their wallpaper, they will leave footprints – some strong, some smudged, and some barely visible. The footsteps symbolize a journey, and so each step can be a story that the child has lived. Once the footprints are made, ask the child what could be written onto each to represent the things they have done through their placement, school, or whatever area you wish to visit. You can use these prints for children who may have to move placement, or school, or to catch the stories that safeguard them.

If paint and the potential 'mess' it could create might be too risky, you can draw faces on the wallpaper or on a piece of paper. For each face, ask the child, 'If you could be anyone, who would you be?' It is important for the child or young person to complete their face them-self if they can (they might choose to draw themselves as a superhero, their parents, their worries or hopes, for example).

A few months ago, a child drew nothing. I was curious and said I couldn't see her or her face, and she replied, with a lovely smile, that it was because her superpower was invisibility!

5

Blocks

BUILDING RELATIONSHIPS

This activity represents the child's story, worries, sadness and confessions. The play supports containment for the child and will support the child from being overwhelmed when engaged in difficult conversations.

A Jenga® set, whether that is a named set or a cheaper version, will ordinarily consist of 48 or 54 wooden blocks, each about the size of your index finger. I provide children with a new set of blocks, so that they can use these blocks for a multitude of interventions. This signifies to them that they are important and deserve new. Other tools I provide to those I work with include colours (texters/pens) and, of course, rolls of wallpaper.

I sometimes use Jenga® blocks to build arches as a skill base exercise, not starting straight away with the formal Jenga® game. Empty the box onto the main table and encourage the child to take an equal share of blocks with their carer and you – ideally you will have 16 or 18 blocks each. With three blocks, build an arch and then invite the child to build another three blocks on top without letting the original arch fall, and then say, 'Let's see how high we can build the tower when we work together!' As each set of three blocks is added to the tower, a series of statements can be made, starting with the easiest ones first, to enable you to set the scene. These can be written down on wallpaper as they are said. As an example I might say, once I have completed a layer, 'I am married to Paula'; on the wallpaper someone will write, 'Richard is married to Paula'. Then the next layer the child might say, 'My best friend is Marla' and the carer or I would write on the wallpaper, 'My best friend is Marla'.

Other questions might include:

What's my name?
Who are my friends?
What do I worry about?

All these responses need to be recorded on the wallpaper lest we forget the value of listening and validating.

When doing this activity you will find that the tower is very wobbly and will probably not get more than five levels high. This is a useful outcome. You can point out to the child, 'Look how wobbly the tower gets when the questions start to get harder, and the tower gets taller.' It's important to point out to the child, too, that 'When the tower falls, it's okay. We can start again!' When the tower falls, the child will generally want to rebuild it. This allows you to reveal more of the child's truth. If you wish to, you could build the foundations more firmly after an initial few tower collapses. Instead of the tower blocks resting on two blocks, the foundations could be made of 20 blocks – the firmer the foundations, the higher we can go. This will help point to the child's need for a strong base, as Abraham Maslow's hierarchy of needs suggests (Maslow 1943).

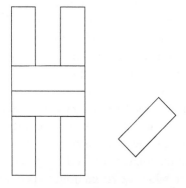

Alternative activity using Jenga® blocks

You can have the child build a house from the Jenga® blocks. Encourage them to identify who lives in the house, and then suggest writing a postcard to those who might live there. For example, build a house that is the child's mother's house. What would they like to tell their mother? Who else might be living there? You could encourage the building of the child's house and then think together what a postcard might say to the child if it was sent to their house. These postcards can develop an understanding of the internal thoughts and worries children may have for the safety of their parent or other family members.

> I was working with an 11-year-old twin. She was worried about her twin who had been placed in a specialized home for children with autistic needs. She had been apart from her twin for several years, but could not talk about her twin as she didn't know what to say. The postcards between the two – one the child and the other what she hoped her sister might say – allowed an opportunity for her to externalize her fears and worries.

Another way you could use the blocks is a simple but fun way of celebrating good news and bad worries. Have the child and carer stand each Jenga® block on its end and create a snake of blocks. Point out how, when working together, the blocks can be placed creatively so that, once they are all in a line, a domino collapse is possible. If this is successful, talk about what else we have done that was successful, and if not successful, what other things feel like that? Involve and observe the relationship between the two (for example, do they help each other, is there discussion between the two, how does the child cope with challenge, and if they cannot manage, how does the carer meet their need?). See how the blocks are spaced, and whether we should worry if the blocks are too far apart. Within a short time, the child and the carer will be talking about the space between those we love, and whether we are in reach of them.

For some children, I may set five blocks in a row on their ends, and the sixth block I would lay face down, then another five blocks on their end and the 12th face down. As the child attempts to knock the bricks down, the face-down blocks stop the continuous flow of the blocks falling. I would then ask the child to pick the face-down block up and respond to what is written on it – it could be a question, a request of a memory or a wishful thinking. Once responded to, we put all the fallen blocks back up on their ends, and the child then watches as the domino effect flows through to the 12th block – which is face down with a question or task written on the side. Once that task is complete, we stand up all the fallen blocks and now we have 17 in a row – the 18th is lying face down and the sequence is repeated until all 54 blocks are ready to fall from one end to the other.

6

Jenga®

THE TOWER BUILDING GAME

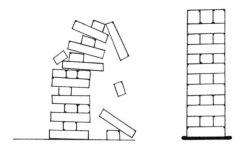

Place three Jenga® blocks on the wallpaper and draw around these. Then build a Jenga® tower, placing the next row of three blocks at a 90-degree turn, just as if you are building a brick wall. Depending on the number of blocks, you will either make 16 or 18 levels in total. Once complete, draw a big circle around the base of the tower you have built, where the edges of the circle touch the edges of the wallpaper. It is at this time that everyone works out the rules for the game, so that when we play, we have agreement to the approach, process and how the game will end. For each rule agreed, write this in the circle that surrounds the tower so that everyone can refer to what was agreed.

Inside the circle, explain that we need to understand the rules because they allow us to be able to play the game fairly, for example:

1. Take it in turns
2. One block at a time
3. You cannot remove a block from the first three rows.

As you begin to play, new rules might need to be made – such as what to do with the block if successfully removed from the tower. This demonstrates that together new approaches can be agreed and old approaches reviewed. This is helpful for children to see that change can be made, and when agreed by all involved, can be successful and safe.

The game itself is full of assessment opportunities. Observing as you play will give you insights into relationship, attachment, play, social skills, cognitive application and attention. I am often surprised as to the reality of family versus the narrative. Carers tell me how their child has a very short attention span, but it is often the carer who struggles to stay on task.

Carers often state that the child doesn't follow rules, but a simple game like Jenga® shows that when rules are broken, little is said and much tolerated – so rules are not necessarily clear, and may not be the boundaries they are designed to be.

It is quite possible to see, in watching the game unfold, the mechanics, the emotions and the relationships within families. Examples include carers who must win at all costs, children who direct and control every moment, carers who overly praise, and those who will not. The game affords the opportunity to identify body language, concentration and exasperation, parallel and engaged play. I would go as far to say that three games of Jenga® will provide enough clues to how those playing are connected or disconnected – not enough for a court assessment, but plenty to gain awareness and plan interventions that will make the difference.

When working with families, we can explore the multiple use of games such as Jenga®. If you are curious about what the child thinks, how they feel, their wishes and their feelings, if you are assessing a child's perception, world or worries, then Jenga® can be very effective. As with the previous approach, get some wallpaper and trace around three blocks to make a template for the base of the Jenga® tower, then draw a circle around the template base so that the edges of the circle touch the edges of the wallpaper. This circle will act as a container for the responses aired during the game.

Write on 20 of the blocks, making up 10 fun questions (like 'If I had a million pounds, what would I buy?') and 10 serious questions (like 'When it's dark I...' or 'If I feel unsafe, I tend to see...' or 'When I dream, I dream of...' or 'I am scared of...'). The questions you choose should match the questions or enquiries you are wanting to affect. They may, for example, be questions about the child's birth family, wishes and feelings, behaviour or hopes and wishes. These 20 question-laden blocks would then be mixed up with the remaining 34 blocks (if using a 54-block set), and you would then build the tower from the template on the wallpaper up. The questions should be randomly built to add to the uncertainty of getting a question.

With the tower built, the questions on the blocks are hidden from view, and the game begins. If the child removes a block and there is no question, the block is placed back on top of the tower and the game continues. Note the reaction of not having a question, which is often disappointment. The next person has their go – say that's you – and you remove a block and there is a question. The question on the block asks, 'My favourite thing to eat is...' and so you respond with 'Sausages are my favourite things for dinner'.

You would then write in the circle your name and that your favourite food is sausages. Once responded to, the block is passed to the child and they might say that their favourite food is McDonald's. You would then write, 'My favourite food is McDonald's', and then the child passes the question on to their carer and they might say, 'My favourite food is pizza'. Again, you would also write that down.

The questions are answered once the blocks with questions are revealed. This is a great way to set opportunities to discuss topics that might be challenging, such as 'My safe place is...', 'When I am angry I...' and 'I would ask my mum...' Each time the questions are answered they are recorded and then written in the circle and so the child's responses can be contained. This is a great way to do 'wishes and feelings work', court work for torn loyalties, and views about care and concepts of 'safe' and 'unsafe'.

I once worked with a young girl of 11, and she told me that the game was not good enough! She demanded that there should be more questions, and so I invited her to add as many questions as she wished. The next time I saw her she had added 34 more questions – some were funny and others insightful. We worked through all the questions she had written and we learned so much about each other.

Another young person was 13 and living in a secure unit. We tried the Jenga® activity and she loved it. We added questions, and one written question was 'You know I am angry when...' I had pulled this question out and so I told her and her carer that 'I go red in the face, and I sulk!' We laughed a little and then she told me that she fidgets when she gets angry. I wrote that down and then looked at the carer, but before the carer could respond, the child told me that she hadn't finished. She said, 'I fidget, and then I rock' (she showed me rocking on her chair and on the balls of her feet). She then said, 'If that doesn't work, I play with my hair and when that doesn't work, you need to watch out, because I blow!!!!!'

This was so helpful to know. This child knew the signs of how she lost her internal control and the warning signs that were present for her. Her carer, a wonderful person, had not realized that there was a pattern and that her child knew about this. She informed her team, and they quickly came up with a response to assist the child in remaining safe – if she fidgeted, change the environment but do not confront; if she was rocking, help her to distract from the triggers by going for a walk or making a cup of tea together; if this was missed and she was playing with her hair, evacuate the room, remove the potential refuelling from other children and young people, and help the child to calm. Within a few short weeks, the incidences of 'explosions' reduced markedly, and within a few months the child stepped down to foster care.

Another child who was placed with carers as his father could not care for him safely refused to talk about his dad or anything connected with him. We played Jenga® and then added questions. He enjoyed this as we shared lives and shared stories. He knew that he could ask questions and even write them on his blocks. A few meetings later, he asked if he could bring his Jenga® blocks to the session and did so. We played question Jenga® and all the questions he had added were about his dad – his worries for his dad, his anger and sadness, his grief and loss. It was amazing and we learned so much. Afterwards, I asked him how he had managed to speak so candidly about his father. He replied with, 'It is a game, and I can ask questions and we have to keep to the rules.' In other words, it is safe!!! 'If I don't want to talk any more, I can bring the tower down.'

Another way of using Jenga® is to introduce colour-coding – so, with a 54-block set, take three colours, let's say green, red and blue. With a marker pen, take 18 blocks and colour the ends green, then 18 blocks and colour them red, and the final 18 blocks, colour these blue. As with the previous approach, get some wallpaper and trace around three blocks to make the template for the base of the Jenga® tower, and then draw a circle around the template base so that the edges of the circle touch the edges of the paper.

This circle will act as a container for the responses aired during the game. Here, the child plays the game on their own, but we support them. The colours all have a rule – the green blocks are there to be questions the child might want to ask about the topic you are talking about in that session. As an example, if you were talking about school and some worries about behaviour there, the child might pull a green end block and ask, 'Why does the teacher in my class always pick on me?' You would write that question in the circle. There may be a few more green blocks, and for each you would write the questions in the circle.

The child might pull a red end block out, which means that the carer or you can ask a question about school – 'When you are in the playground, what are the main difficulties for you?' This question is written on the wallpaper and placed with the other questions.

Then turn to the blue blocks, for empathy and emotions. Ask the child to take a moment and put themselves in the shoes of another person present, in the school scenario, as a teacher or another child caught up in the event. This is helpful as the child starts to consider how others might think, feel and do. By affording this opportunity the child might appreciate the situation, and may change their behaviour or their engagement as they understand how and why others do what they do.

7

The Boat

I have used the concept of a therapeutic journey to talk about hopes and fears, and when beginning to work with children and young people, one of the first tasks is to give confidence and surety. A visual approach to this is the boat activity.

Ask the child you are working with to draw a boat – it can be any size and any style. (A few years ago a child of seven drew a shark-styled boat and it was brilliant.) Once the boat has been drawn ask the child to draw themselves on the boat and anybody they would like to be with on the boat, although they can, of course, be on their own. Then draw the water that the boat is floating on and invite the child to draw sea creatures and anything else – other children have included scuba divers, SpongeBob SquarePants and his friends, and even plastic bottles.

Ask the child how the boat is kept in the same place on the sea if you don't want the current or the wind to move the boat away.

Children will quickly tell you that the boat needs an anchor to be safe – so draw an anchor from the cable attached to the boat to the bottom of the seabed. The anchor weight needs to be visual. Ask the child if the anchor is heavy enough to hold the boat steady and still. Hopefully the child will tell you that the anchor has to grip rocks on the seabed to be strong and if so, draw the rocks. At this point, it is helpful to ask the child who the anchors are in their life, the people who keep them safe. If identified, write the names on the anchor; if not, explore with the child the people who have care or responsibility for them.

Next, explain that the therapeutic work with the child can sometimes be a bit like the weather – it can be calm and fun, but other times windy and stormy. If the boat has a strong anchor, it will be safe, and the sea, if it becomes stormy, cannot hurt the boat or the people on it because the anchor will keep it still. I have had children talk about needing stronger anchors, or that they have no anchors at school, or in contact, but that they need them.

If you do have a situation where the child you are working with seems unsure, or resisting, try this boat activity, and when it comes to a missing anchor, explore where one might be found – it may be you for the first few months, and then new ones are forged or old ones renewed.

8

Squiggles

Donald Winnicott, an English paediatrician and psychoanalyst, contributes to much of my approach with traumatized children (1965) – I try hard to hold the pain of those I work with in the hope that they will feel safe and know that I will not be overwhelmed by them. Winnicott's squiggles are a helpful way to begin to make relationships with children, a perfect opportunity to show that on our own we make little sense, but together we can make all the sense in the world. I would recommend reading a very short but excellent paper, 'Winnicott Squiggles', which is downloadable by visiting the Squiggle Foundation. Invite the child and carer to play this game – on a piece of paper or wallpaper. Get a texter and draw a line that is just a free-flow shape. Then invite the child and the carer to think together on how they might add to the drawing so that we might recognize something. Hopefully they will have lots of ideas, and when they have chosen a particular one, either the child or the carer might complete the drawing.

Once you have modelled the interaction, invite the child to draw a squiggle, and then you and the carer think together so the child can see that you can work well, and when either you or the carer have agreed something, complete the drawing and ask the child if they recognize it.

Once done, the carer draws a squiggle and then you and the child discuss together, and once agreed, you or the child complete the picture. If we are trying to make sense of something, we often find it hard by ourselves, but if we share the something together, we might find a way through. This simple activity works so well; it can be funny, it can be thoughtful, and as you do more and more, the storytelling improves relationships.

When working with children who are hard to engage, it might be that the child doesn't trust you. Some children who have been therapized to the point of saturation become experts at shutting down attempts to engage, as such interventions feel dangerous for them. I have a lot of experiences with children who are experts at shutting down adults, but the use of squiggles can make the difference. A few children I have worked with take their time to attachment dance with me. We may often step on each other's toes, but after a while we learn the steps to become at ease with each other. In my case, this would be play, and squiggles work well.

> Meet Michaela. At 11 years old, she was very hard to engage; she had been therapized to the point of saturation, and had managed to fend off all attempts to help her. She was the same with me, until we found squiggles. She loved the idea of these, and three sessions later she was not letting me go past squiggles. On my way back from the third session, I was contacted by the social worker to be told that the sessions needed to be stopped.

A practice-experienced belief that I hold dear is the following.

Can you hold me safe?

The first time you see a child for a therapeutic intervention they are interested, they want to please you and they want to meet your needs. The second time, the child might be more curious about you and need to know what you want from them. And the third time is where the child needs to see if they can still get rid of you! The challenge, refusal or arousal is often portrayed in their challenging behaviour.

Sadly, many therapeutic workers see this third time as the child not being ready, that they feel unsafe, and the therapy would not be in their interest. The reality is that they are saying to you, 'Okay, I like you, but can you manage me, can you keep me safe?' So to walk away is the worst thing we can do.

In Michaela's case, I was able to persuade the social worker of another visit. At the fourth visit I attended the house and she met me in the driveway with the words 'I am ready now'. We went on to do some amazing work using narrative trees, behaviour trees and the Ishikawa model. All these need a modicum of trust, and it is possible, if we meet the fundamental need of showing children we can be safe. This same child said to her carers and to me words to the effect of, 'If I am in school or at home and I don't feel safe, I try people out to see if I am safe; if they can keep me safe, I am safe. If they can't, I am not safe; I become an angry animal, an angry lion, an angry me'.

9

Story Stones

There are many different ways to use story stones. You can buy coloured stones, word stones and story-making stones such as Pirate Dice™. I am notoriously keen to make as much as I can from scratch with the child – these self-made tools mean much more to the relationship and those engaged. You don't need to buy anything for this activity, and I have found most children really enjoy it. If you live near a beach, or perhaps an area where you can collect groups of five thumb-sized stones, that is all you need. You could always take the child to a local garden centre and invite them to pick their own stones if you are really unable to find some in the local area. You can, of course, use pebbles and riverbed stones. The stones do not have to be big – the size of a Jenga® block would be ideal – and if you are stuck, use a Jenga® block!

Think of a theme – this might be friends, court, contact, school and/or emotions. Then, with four of the stones, use a permanent marker pen and write a word on each. If you are talking about contact, you might choose 'family', 'play', 'feelings' and 'safe', or if you were thinking about school, you might choose 'teacher', 'bully', 'play' and 'class'. The fifth stone is left blank, and this is for the child to pick a word to be written on it – this could be 'scared', 'worried', 'help', and so on.

Once all the stones have a word on them, the child can then arrange them in any order they choose. When they are ready, they can tell you a story using all five words about the theme agreed. This activity, although short and easy, can provide the best of communication. I have often found myself listening to some very difficult memories and some sad experiences when other forms of communication have proved unhelpful.

Story stones can also be used for fun, and it is always good to try them out first on lighter subjects. I often use stones with 'fun', 'circus', 'elephants' and 'trapeze' written on them. My fifth stone has the title of a film – in this case *The Greatest Showman* – and the child has to guess the film. We then take turns guessing characters, books, TV and famous people.

Why don't you try it now? If your favourite place to be is the seaside, ask the child to write on four of the stones words connected to your favourite place. These might be 'sea', 'beach', 'food' and 'sun'. Then you can write on the fifth stone a word of your choice – let's say you write 'boat'. You would then arrange the words, so you could put 'beach', 'sea', 'boat', 'food' and then 'sun'. Now the story is told in this order:

> My favourite place to go is the *beach*, but not any beach. I love going to the beach in Morfa Nefyn. The place is quiet and peaceful, with only a few people there, and the *sea* is so shallow that I can paddle out to the boats that lazily bob up and down with the tide going out. My *boat* is a little white one, with a small sail and a little motor, and once we are all in it, we can sail to the next beach where there is a beachside pub called Ty Coch, and we can have *food* and soak up the *sun*.

Think of the themes and the potential for this activity in communication. It can be, as it has been for me, a brilliant way to talk about things that are sometimes so big and worrying but that don't need to be if we break them down into bite-size chunks. And, by the way, I find that five subjects to address is a good number of topics to use in the sessions.

10

The Box Game/
Paddocks/Squares

The box game allows for nine different stories to be told, and is a great way of helping to bring subjects into conversations and to deal with the thoughts and worries that might be present.

On a piece of paper, draw 16 dots in a pattern of four dots by four dots.

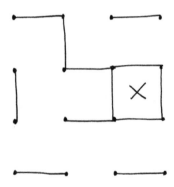

Once each player has taken a colour pen, explain how the game works. For each go, the player joins two dots together, either horizontally or vertically. Make sure that everyone knows that joining dots diagonally is not allowed as we want to make squares and not triangles. As the dots are joined, it will become possible to then draw a line that connects three lines to make a square. Whoever makes the square will win that box, and they put their initials in it. Once each of the nine potential boxes is complete, the game ends and we can count up how many boxes each person won. The one with the most boxes wins.

This is a quick and lovely game that many children and adults enjoy...but do not have more than 16 dots in each game as it can get repetitive. Lots of quick games work better. After playing a few times, it might be helpful to think of a theme that the intervention is engaged with – friends, emotions, school, home and/or family. Draw the dots again, and this time, if a square is completed, invite the person who secured the box to say something to do with the theme – for example, with a theme such as 'family', the stories or memories shared might be about a mother or father.

As this is a game, children are thinking less about their answers and more about winning. Therefore, we can talk about worries, thoughts and feelings in a fun way and with less inhibition. I have been amazed at what children will talk about within this framework – and that is crucially what it becomes, a reflection of a theme and the understanding of the child's engagement within this.

> I learned about engagement from a 14-year-old boy, who was struggling at home. We played the box game, and he asked if, when he won a box, he could say something about school. I was curious about this so I agreed, and so I would talk about my work and his carer would talk about her work. We began to play and then he won a box. I asked him about school, and he wrote, 'I am stealing things from children at school, and I can't stop' in his box. Ordinarily his carer would have reacted to this and it would quickly become a rupture as he became aggressive to be safe and she became angry at his behaviour and struggled to hide her disappointment. As this was part of the game, whatever was shared was contained within the boxes on the paper, and once we concluded the whole nine boxes, his carer had got past her initial 'shock' responses and was much calmer and able to think with him about the problems he had at school.

I found referring to this instance very helpful, to have a way that children and carers could have difficult conversations once the initial reaction had been contained; the boxes as containment were tremendously effective. We continued to use the box game in most sessions, and I use them regularly when working with children and families today.

11

Balloons and Bubbles

Starting off with different fun ways of sharing difficult topics or secrets is a great way to build trust and relationships for children to share. Many children, especially those aged from 3 to 11, find it hard to say certain things or certain words as they may be rude, might get them into trouble for saying something, or maybe they have heavy secrets. Using simple things such as balloons or bubbles can be really useful, and the following ideas may be helpful.

Purchase a pack of normal party balloons and set aside six. Then ask the child if they would like to whisper any worries, sad things or questions into the neck of the balloon that you are about to inflate. Once they have whispered into the neck of the balloon, blow it up and then tie the neck so that the balloon stays inflated. If the child is fine with loud pops, invite them to pop the balloon, but challenge them to shout louder than the pop of the balloon the words they whispered into the balloon – this is akin to a primal scream, but it works well.

I normally demonstrate this first, and it is always funny. Once shown and encouraged, permission to scream out with the burst of the balloon is welcomed. Once the words are out, write them on the wallpaper and invite the child to either draw a red circle around the words so that they can keep the information safe and unvisited, or they can draw a blue cloud, which means we can explore further.

For children who do not like loud noises, you can use bubbles. Purchase a bubble solution. Then add a little washing-up liquid or sugar to the liquid to make the bubbles stronger. Ask the child to think of any worries, words or secrets that are difficult to talk about, and then invite them to blow bubbles through the stick hole into the air – the bubbles materialize and then you, the carer and the child try and catch them without letting the bubbles burst.

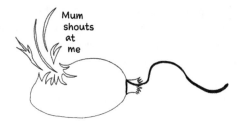

For each bubble that doesn't pop, it means that we can catch them and hold any worries that the child might have, and then invite them to tell us about them. As with the balloons, write these on the wallpaper, using the red circle or blue cloud idea around the words you can safeguard (red) or explore (blue). If you, the child or anyone involved in this communication work do not want to talk about something, draw a red circle around the words on the wallpaper. As an example:

> Mummy and Daddy used to get very angry towards each other and sometimes Daddy would be hit by Mummy.

The child can draw a red circle around the above sentence. The red circle means that we cannot talk about it until the child alters the red circle by drawing a blue cloud over the red circle – thus indicating their willingness or need to talk about the subject recently red-circled but now open for discussion.

This safeguarding on what can and cannot be discussed at that moment in time is just as effective a tool for us therapists. There may well be times when we do not want to answer or narrate on a subject at a time the child might wish to – so we can simply draw a red circle around it and it would have the same rules as above. It is a perfect way to acknowledge something, but also to contain and hold it until we are ready.

12

Telephone

This should take many of you back to your childhood, the idea of linking two yogurt pots (in my day, two tins) with a length of string to act as a telephone line. I am sure that I do not need to talk you through it, but just in case... Get two paper cups or empty yoghurt containers and a long piece of string. Make this telephone set-up in session, with the child helping you. Make a hole in the centre of the base of each cup, and on one cup thread through the string, tying off with a knot to secure the string at the base of the inner cup. Tie the other end of the string to the other cup and secure this with a knot so the connection is secure.

Then, take it in turns to use as a telephone or walkie-talkie and hold a conversation – 'Roger and Out!!'

This method is brilliant when working with younger children who may find eye contact difficult in intense conversations. If the child is hiding behind a kitchen island or by the rear patio door and the adult is in a different room, the intensity of the discussion is tempered by the distance and 'fun' of saying 'Roger and Out!'

I remember working with a seven-year-old who did not want to talk about the hurt that one of his parents had done to him. He was cautious as he didn't want his mum or dad to get cross with him for saying something about them.

With the cups, the conversation and its limits are completely in the gift of the young person for when they say 'Roger and Out!' for the final time. This approach can help children feel confident to tell their stories, so they can make sense of their own world.

13

Air Balloon

This is one of the most effective tools that I use, and is loosely influenced by Violet Oaklander's 'Boat in the Storm' drawing (2015) and the Three Houses in the Signs of Safety programme from Andrew Turnell and Steve Edwards (1999). Many young people find it hard to talk about sad and traumatic events as it feels too close to the hurt.

In 2004, I started using a simple process to separate the child from their story. To try and create an opportunity for them to have a view of their journey without being present in the description or narrative, we would often use the term 'helicopter' or 'bird's eye' view. The air balloon was developed to give this opportunity of separation, but also to be fun and easy to replicate.

Over the last 13 years I have trained tens of thousands of professionals to engage with children using narrative approaches, communication tools and relational intervention; there are many books now about the Rose Model of Therapeutic Life Story Work that describe this incredibly effective intervention. Within the training, students are required to demonstrate practical applications of their learning to direct work, and to be approved, they have to present examples of practice with the young people they are engaged with. A majority of these students choose to present the air balloon as the tool that they found most useful.

Let's go ballooning!

On the wallpaper or a large piece of paper, draw an air balloon floating in a clear blue sky – the air balloon should be placed in the top left corner so that you can take it on a journey across the sky. Ask the child if you can draw them in the basket that is under the air balloon, but don't draw any facial expressions. Next, ask who they would like to take in the air balloon with them. It can't be you as you will be the narrator and facilitator; it might be a friend, a carer or a family member. Once settled on, draw them in the basket as well – don't worry if the child wants a toy or an animal (one of my young people wanted 13 rabbits!). Again, leave the faces blank so that you can fill these in once everything else is drawn.

With the child and the friend (for example) in the air balloon, explain that the weather is calm and that the air balloon is still. Ask how the child is feeling, and draw this on the child's face in the basket. Then do the same for the friend in the basket, and reflect on how that feeling is felt at other times.

Ask the child to look over the basket to the floor below. Ask what they can see. Sometimes I ask where they would like to be and what they would like to look at. Children often talk about seeing their birth family home, or Disneyland, the Loch Ness Monster and so on. As they explain what they see, draw it on the ground, and encourage them to describe what they see in detail.

> One child I worked with told me that the air balloon was in the town where his mum lived, and that we were looking at her house. All of a sudden, he exclaimed that he could see his sister and it wasn't fair that she could still live with his mum and he couldn't. This was the reason I was working with him, to talk about the fact that social services had decided that he had to stay in care.

On the wallpaper towards the right, draw a storm, using clouds and lightning, and then explain that the air balloon has to travel through the storm and that there is no alternative. Draw the air balloon in the middle of the storm and show it distressed. Have the two figures in the basket, the child and their friend, and ask how the child might be feeling if they were in the storm. Talk about the worry and the danger, and think with the child about how their friend might be feeling. I have, on some occasions, explained how I might feel if I was in an air balloon in a storm, to give support of being scared and anxious.

Ask the child to look over the side of the basket and down to the ground. If it was scary in the sky, was there anything on the ground that would have been scary for them, too? Draw what they describe.

So many children have told me about the worries they carry, or the 'hurting house' (where they have been hurt by others) or 'school'. It is so effective. Then, draw on the far-right side of the wallpaper a beautiful sun, and draw the air balloon enjoying the sun.

> For the child who wanted to see his family home, his unsafe scary place was his grandad's home and his safe place was his foster home. I can still recall the smile that appeared on his foster carer's face as she heard, really heard for the first time, that her child felt safe with her.

Explain that the air balloon has survived the storm and is now calm and sunning itself. Ask how the child is feeling now, and draw that emotion on the child's face in the basket. Then ask how their friend is feeling, and finally, ask the child to look over the basket to the ground, and to describe their safe place. Once more draw this as the child describes it.

This is a good activity – with all the descriptions written in the clouds around the basket, it means that all is honoured and recorded.

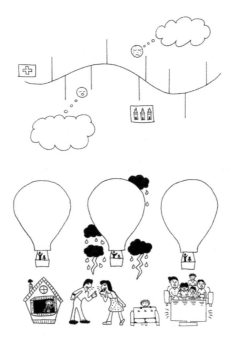

14

Arrows

HIGH EXPECTATION/LOW EXPECTATION

This activity is really helpful for a carer and a child where they are stuck with the challenge of behaviours and expectations that over-whelm them as individuals and prevent them being as one. It is a simple process, but yields great conversational opportunities.

On a piece of paper, draw a large double-headed arrow. It needs to be large to be able to write in it, and once done, in the left-hand arrowhead write 'Younger than'; in the right-hand arrow head write 'Older than'. In the middle of the arrow, write 'Age okay'. I often write 'Immature', 'Mature' and 'Pseudo-mature', but these words may be too difficult or adult for some children – it really depends on the child and how you have developed the relationship so far.

> I can remember a 19-year-old I worked with, and we used 'Baby behaviour', 'Nothing to worry about here behaviour' and finally 'Older than I am behaviour', and this worked beautifully when thinking about spitting, tantrums, smoking, vaping, lying and sexual behaviour.

With the arrow complete, if you are only with the child's carer, ask them to write down as many of the behaviours that the child shows – good, bad and in between – these need to be scattered all over the piece of paper. If doing this with the child on their own, ask them to do the same. Sometimes I will do this with the carer and the child together at the same time, but this doesn't always work as well. If I were you, do them separately, and then bring the pieces of paper together and discuss with them both.

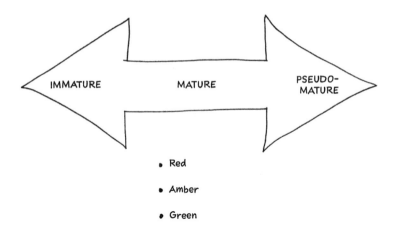

- Red
- Amber
- Green

Let us keep with the carer for now. They may have written behaviours such as swearing, stealing, biting, vaping, having a girl/boyfriend, drinking alcohol, hanging round the bus stop, looking at porn. When completed, I would ask the carer to decide which behaviours were 'Younger than', 'Age okay' and 'Older than', and draw a line to show where each behaviour sits. Again, do the same for the child. If you put them together, you will see where there is agreement and where there is conflict. You will also see the high and/or low expectations of the carer, which is particularly helpful when working with children with attention deficit hyperactivity disorder (ADHD), autism spectrum disorder (ASD) and attachment disorder.

The next stage is to decide what priority there is for each behaviour. This is done using a traffic light process. Ask the carer which of the behaviours are intolerable for them, and mark these with a red dot; then which ones are not wanted but tolerable, and mark these with an amber dot; finally, which behaviours are acceptable, and mark these green. Repeat this with the child, and again, see what is agreeable and what is in conflict. It is simple but effective in singling out the areas to concentrate on and what can wait. It helps families to think together and compromise so that there is time to develop healthier environments for all.

The arrows activity is effective both in school and at home, and I hope you will find this communication skill helpful.

15

Bar Charts

I would expect that you, as you are reading this chapter, are thinking of other things such as home, health, your job and your family. When you are engaged in an activity, you may find that there are other demands for your attention, or that a thought won't stop its presentation and so will drag you from listening or paying attention to the current situation. This is often referred to as 'preoccupation'. If your preoccupation is very demanding, you might start to misread, to skip or to give up reading this chapter altogether.

What is distracting you from what you are doing right now? What is taking you away from this book? What is demanding your attention and so conflicting with your current activity?

For this activity, draw a tall rectangle (a bar chart), and once done, write '0%' at the bottom and '100%' at the top. Now, identify what you are thinking about that has nothing to do with what you are doing in this exercise. What might be distracting you? It might be work, family, hunger or thoughts that need your attention. Note these from the bottom moving upwards. As an example, sitting here, in a coffee shop, I am thinking about my young people and the New Year restart; I have this manuscript to get to the publishers in two days; and I have recently been informed of another child I may need to work with. I would write these from the bottom and pile them upwards, using up the space in my bar chart.

Once you have completed your acknowledgements of preoccupation, rate from 0–100% how much you are preoccupied. How much is left is the opportunity to be present, attentive and receptive to new information. In my example, at least 25% of my brain is non-receptive as it is already committed elsewhere.

It is important to know that we can still pay attention despite high levels of preoccupation, but the energy and concentration might mean that we are so much more tired at the end of the day. Think of the last time you had a hard day – you are buzzing with response-ready action and, at the end of the day or shift, you get home and the night or your time just escapes you as your body and brain scream, 'Enough is enough!' For those of you who are carers, this is something you will recognize so easily as you manage your exhausted children who appear on the doorstep after a day at school trying to hold it all in! The higher your percentage of preoccupation, the harder you need to work and make sense of things in the moment, and the more exhausted you are at the end. Now, think of this bar chart as your brain. The fuller it is, the more capacity is being used up, and there is less room for anything else to be attended to.

> Imagine this 12-year-old with a history of child sexual exploitation. I tried to engage her in thinking about her past. Each time I tried she would react with small behaviour traits that said 'I can't talk about this, it is too dangerous and too scary' but that presented as shouting, hitting and anger. On the fourth session she said to me, 'I know why I need to work with you, Richard.' I said, 'What's happened?' She replied, 'We were doing bar charts in school and while I was in school doing bar charts, I was thinking about lots of different things, and I managed to work out that there was too much in my brain.' I asked if she could help me understand what she had worked out.
>
> She asked me to draw a bar chart on the paper we used to talk about her life (I used rolls of wallpaper, so that we could develop a pictorial tapestry of the child's journey). I did as she asked. Once done, she asked me to write in the bar chart what she had been thinking about. She said, 'I was thinking about my mum.' So I had to write the following down in the bar chart – 'My mum had alcohol issues. She'd get drunk, she'd fall, often she'd be sick.' She then said that she 'would make sure mum was okay'. She'd look after her two younger siblings and then, at night time, she'd keep coming downstairs to make sure that mum was still okay. That was her role in the family, to make sure that mum was okay and to parent the little children.
>
> I asked if there was a reason for thinking about this in class, and she told me that this was a constant thought (and that

she was waiting for the police to come to tell her that her mum was dead) – that nobody was there to look after her, and that it would be her fault if this did happen as she should be there to care for her mother.

She then asked me to make the bar chart taller. I did, and then she told me that she was also thinking about her younger brother. Her brother had been adopted three years previously (this child and her younger sisters had gone into care and her baby brother went straight to an adopted family placement). Her brother's new parents promised that they would write to her every six months so she would know that he was okay. They had never, ever written to her. She held this boy in her head because she could not afford to let her brother disappear.

She then added her fears about her birth dad. He was in prison for assaulting her mother and her mother's brother. Her social worker told her that her dad was being released. The little girl was afraid he might find where her mum was living and go to her home and assault her again, and she wouldn't be there to protect her. She reached over me and her carer, and she closed the bar chart but left a little space at the top. She said, 'With all this in my head, I only had this much left to learn maths.'

To really understand this, complete your own bar chart and write from the bottom upwards what is preoccupying you, and each area will take away your space to be present for reading or continuing to read this. Once complete, draw a line above the last words to see how much of you is left to learn, act, play or to be.

If you have been reading this book but not doing the activities, this is one to do, so have a go. Take a moment and grab a pen, draw a bar chart and consider what competing thoughts you have in your head at this moment. For me, as I write this book, I am bombarded with case work, health issues and the deadline fast arriving for this manuscript! How about you? Write these in your bar chart from the bottom towards the top, and stop once you have completed your list. For me, right now, I am 25% preoccupied. If you were to think of the bar chart as your brain capacity, how much of your bar chart have you filled, and how much do you have left?

My 12-year-old was 90% full and struggling with school, the

current challenges in her world and her placement. I asked her how therapeutic life story work would help, and she said that my job was to write down all the things that she was worried about on the wallpaper. We could talk about it and think how to understand and find out more together. An accurate thing to record is that the young person said, 'We can write it down on the wallpaper so that I don't have to carry it around any more'.

If you have ever had a worry that you couldn't stop thinking about, that would surface when you tried to do everything to keep it down, this is the reality for many of our traumatized children. I want to be more helpful here and relate my own experience of this. My job takes me to Australia from the UK often, and on one occasion I was finding it hard to keep up with the demands that I put on myself during the early years of my independent work (and, truth be known, still try and do too much!). I had arrived in Parramatta, Sydney, after a long flight from the UK, and although exhausted, I couldn't sleep and so continued to write up a report I was required to provide within the calendar week. At 3 am, I decided I needed to get some sleep and so placed the documents and my computer in the room safe.

The next thing I remember was hearing heavy knocking on my bedroom door. I had overslept, and I was due to catch a flight to Perth – the driver was at the door urging me to get sorted. I rushed my stuff together and dressed as quickly as possible. On the way to the airport, I wasn't as worried about flying as I usually am. I got on the plane and again, unusually, I wasn't thinking that this was to be my last flight (I have an irrational fear of flying). The plane left the runway and all of a sudden, my brain caught up – I couldn't remember taking my computer or the documents out of the safe. The four-hour flight was a reflection of my disappearing career, as I fantasized how I could get back to pick the computer and papers – maybe a night flight, maybe a courier? I then worried that someone might find the paperwork and I would be de-registered for poor practice. I didn't panic at every bump of turbulence, I wasn't looking to get a quick Jack Daniel's to self-medicate my unease of being in a metal tin at 37,000 feet, I didn't really register that we had a missed landing and a go-around – I was just preoccupied with the contents of the safe and the dire ramifications of my folly.

When the plane landed in Perth, I ran to the baggage hall and was eventually reunited with my bag. I ripped it open (literally) and there, at the top of my clothes, was the laptop and documents. I burst into tears and the relief was momentous... I am not comparing this to a child's trauma, but merely trading the reality of preoccupation. It limits you and tires you out. It can overwhelm and develop a creative and sometimes destructive sense of self – in my situation, a reality that I was not good enough, and so on.

So, for every child I work with, we draw bar charts to identify the worries that get in the way of thinking together; this allows us to acknowledge and put to one side these worries, accepting that there is nothing we can do at that moment but to respect the worries we carry. Communicating our preoccupation allows us to externalize the weight we carry and shares the burden with those who listen.

Imagine a school class – most of the children are alert and ready to learn. Many children have little to worry them and have the capacity to be present, and over the next hour or so, they process all that is there to learn. In the class, though, there may well be a child who has much in their heads – hunger, worries, memories, ghosts of the past, fear of the present – each takes up space in their brain, therefore adding to preoccupation and taking away from their ability to be present. The teaching starts and before long the child may become overwhelmed; they have no space for this learning, and as the information is overflowing their reservoir capacity, they become aware of the disconnect. The child can't hear any more, they are no longer available to the learning process, but they may see that other children seem to be managing.

Fear evolves as the child starts to realize that they are not able to stay on task, and what if the teacher was to ask questions? The other children might see that they were not as clever as them, so what can the child do to feel safe? The simple response is to make space. They may need their monster to create chaos in order to survive – the impacted child may start to nudge another child, start to throw things at another child or start to make noises in the class. They may need to disrupt the class so that they're not exposed as being weak, stupid, not good enough or similar shame.

If that works the first time, and if that works the second and the third, why wouldn't they do the same thing when the same threat occurs? Just as you and I would do, if we know something works and it works, why do a different action? We would do what works!

Using glasses of water to help children, teachers and carers to understand the impact of preoccupation on the child attending is a great visual. If you can, get three glasses from the cupboard, then fill one of the glasses with water so it is 20% full, one glass until it is 60% full, and finally the last glass filled with water to 90%.

The 20% full glass represents the settled pupil in the class, the 60% full is the teacher's glass containing the lesson to be shared and the 90% full glass represents the very preoccupied child.

As the children are in the class, the teacher's 60% lesson is 'poured' into the glass holding 20% water; the glass can receive the 60% lesson (water) and not overflow – have a go. You can see that the child can attend and manage the lesson, and as they understand the learning, this reduces the level of their glass, and eventually it will revert to the 20% level.

Now, replace the water in the second glass back to the level of 60% (the lesson); get hold of the third glass that has 90% full of water – this represents the pupil who is greatly preoccupied – and pour the second glass 'lesson' into this glass. Very quickly, the glass is full, yet water is still pouring in and overflowing as the lesson continues (sorry about the mess) – this represents the reality for the preoccupied child in the classroom, so preoccupied that the lesson being taught is not connecting and the child is no longer able to manage the situation.

For many preoccupied children in this situation, they are fully aware they are no longer able to listen, and they look around them to see if other children seem to be struggling. Dr Perry refers to the concept of 'flocking' – as the child hopes to see others feeling as they are, if they can, they can feel a little easier, as they can see 'it's not just me' (Perry and Winfrey 2021). If what they see confirms they are on their own, that they are isolated in their struggle, this might need a panic and potential shame response. The child might conclude that their best option is to let their 'monster' play – to protect them by causing mayhem and being sent out of the class they are not managing.

Communicating that the child is feeling overwhelmed in the classroom can be very difficult for them – how do they do this without the potential for shame, embarrassment or risk? For my sessions with children, filling in a bar chart at the beginning affords the opportunity to provide the child with time to express their worries, and so reduce the preoccupation to allow for the 60% lesson from the teacher.

I am, like many of you, very busy, and so, when I visit a child to do therapeutic work, before I leave my car I will draw a bar chart and write all the worries and problems that I can identify in it. This allows me to make space in my head so as to be available to the children I am there to help...much like a shopping list, I know it is there, and I can come back to it when I need to.

Think about a foster child, after a hard day at school. They get home and their carer says something like, 'Go to your bedroom and take your school clothes off; put the dirty clothes in the laundry basket, have a wash, put your play stuff on, and then come down to the kitchen.' This child might get to their bedroom and will not know what to do next – what's happened? They haven't done anything because they haven't managed to hear anything other than the initial instruction.

They are now upstairs thinking, 'What am I supposed to be doing?' The carer gets angry because they've not done what they have been told; the child is already anticipating the anger, and may need to create another event so that the carer will forget what they told them to do in the first place.

Remember one of the children we spoke of earlier in this book – 'When you are at school or at home and you don't know if you are safe, you have to try people out, to see if they can keep me safe. If they can keep me safe, I am safe. If they can't, well then, I must keep myself safe. I become an angry lion, an angry animal, an angry me.'

16

Roller Coaster

Think of this in a different way. How many of you like roller coasters? You're in the roller coaster car with all your favourite people in it. You've got this massive climb to the top of the ride, then a steep drop, followed by the loop-the-loops projecting you to the end. As you sit in the car, and before the ride starts, a fairground worker comes over and places the safety bar against your lap and the laps of those sharing the car with you. What do you do next?

Well, with my lack of trust and need for self-preservation, I would check the bar is in place. I would give it a real shake and expect it to stay securely fixed. If it does, I feel safe and I can enjoy the ride. What if, on trying the bar, it sprang loose and no longer secured me or those important to me? It would mean I am no longer safe. How would you react? I know I would have to get myself safe. There is no difference to this need to feel safe and how our hurt children in care need to feel safe in the care of carers – the roller coaster is their placement, and just like the bar to keep us safe, that is the role of the carers, to provide a secure base where the child is safe no matter what occurs.

Imagine that you are a child in the care of a foster carer and you notice problems around the family; your parent figures are arguing more and more, being in the environment is like walking on eggshells and it feels unsafe. Every so often you might wonder if your carer is able to keep you safe. So, you may try out the bar (carer), and you might revert to previous behaviour to see if your bar (carer) can keep you safe.

If the carer responds by saying, 'Hey, it's okay, there are a few worries but nothing that will stop me keeping you safe', then that might be good enough for you to acknowledge you are safe and the safety bar is working. If, rather than reacting positively, the carer replies by saying, 'Don't you start, can't you see I am struggling? Get out of my way, I can't cope with you as well right now.' Well then, there is only you who can keep you safe, and so you go back to the behaviours that have served you well.

With all these cases presented, I hope that these activities help to encourage the sharing of stories as they are worked through. This will then support the narrative towards a child's trauma recovery. In telling their story, we can bear witness and hold the child's pain while we share other stories of those involved in their journey. This provides the time and space to assist in reframing the narrative as a more informed and therapeutic story that has dealt with shame, guilt, confusion, anger and the unknown. All of us are a collection of stories that represent what we were to who we are. In understanding our story, we can move forward to a future not constrained or defined by an unresolved past. Stories are meaning, stories help us make sense, stories are something to lean on.

17

Monsters and Ghosts

The truth is that monsters are real and ghosts are real too.
They live inside us, and sometimes they win.

(KING 1977)

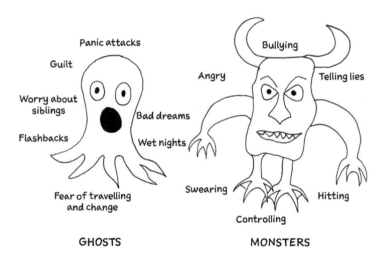

GHOSTS

Panic attacks
Guilt
Worry about siblings
Flashbacks
Bad dreams
Wet nights
Fear of travelling and change

MONSTERS

Bullying
Angry
Telling lies
Swearing
Controlling
Hitting

The concept of trauma for me has always been the presence of unre-solved residuals left afterwards and not the trauma event itself. If we all were present at a traumatic event, each of us will experience the event in a unique way. In short, what we are left with afterwards will vary in how we manage our emotional, physical, cognitive, spiritual or sensory reaction, as we are all unique, so our traumas and our stories are also unique. The important word within some trauma definitions is 'residual' – what remains, the unresolved hurt. I explain it as our ghosts of the past.

I have residue of trauma in my life, but I have accepted and made my peace with these – in short, I live alongside them, and am not defined by them. I also have unresolved issues, and these do overwhelm me and I am wary of them. The monsters and ghosts exercise affords the opportunity to support children to identify their trauma and their ghosts, and in doing so, understand their past trauma (ghosts) and allow the monsters in their behaviour to fall away.

Why the concept of ghosts? If you would like to, get a sheet of paper and draw a ghost on the far left. Next, consider three words that might describe your ghost, words like 'memories', 'insubstantial', 'corner of the eye movement', 'frightening' or 'unwelcome'. Next, think of a moment in your life that sometimes resurfaces to your present – it could be a good memory or a difficult one. Where does this memory come from? How is it still there? And, more importantly, what are you feeling at this moment and how are you coping with this? What is happening in your heart and your body?

At the end of this exercise, think what it would be like if you were not consciously seeking this memory, but that the memory was constantly seeking you. Ghosts are real.

Alongside trauma, we have the manifestation of its impact – while we are in a playful mood, get another piece of paper...on the far-left side draw a monster. Once you have drawn your picture, think of three words that might describe this monster. These could include 'angry', 'dangerous', 'overwhelming' or maybe 'safe' and 'protective'. Ask yourself this – 'Do I have a monster in me?' – and put the word 'Yes' or 'No' next to the description. If you do not have a monster in you, I would be worried about you! It might be when you get cross and shout at someone, or you swear and instantly realize that was not appropriate. It could be due to road rage or through running away or towards the stimuli of the moment – you might understand it as a reaction to your loss of internal control, where you are now vulnerable and scared, so you respond to this by subconsciously responding for survival.

Our monster serves a purpose, in the main to protect us when we lose our internal control, when we are vulnerable and fearful (although we might not understand this at the time). If it helps, think of it as your safety valve, your personal failsafe!

This can be a default, a go-to at times of stress, but its purpose is to push the threat away, to gain space to reclaim control and assess the risk. Does this work for you? On the paper next to 'Yes', describe your monster when it responds, and then think of the outcome of your monster's appearance. It certainly works for me; despite my emotions afterward, I can understand that when all else fails, I must protect my 'self'. Finally, when your monster has done what it needed to and resided back in your space, think about how you would feel then.

You might feel shameful, embarrassed, relieved or exhausted. Finally, place these emotional aftermaths next to the monster traits. In both the ghosts and the monster pieces of paper you now have a sequence of responses to overwhelming events – ghosts are real, and monsters are real too.

In the early 2000s, Kathy Stansbury and Michael Harris found that children who live in chaotic environments learn techniques to keep them safe; these techniques are coping strategies that are in the main 'defence-based' (Stansbury and Harris 2000). If the chaos they experience continues and becomes a constant, these strategies become behaviour. For many traumatized children, carrying the hurt of the past enables them to quickly see threat, and in the fear that results, they revert to their default behaviour to protect their self. For highly traumatized children who have had monstrous things happen to them, their survival behaviour can seem monstrous. It is hard sometimes to remember that what the child is doing is for safety and survival, but it is all driven by the past and based on a 'what works principle'.

In my work with traumatized children and young people who have, as part of their defence systems, aggression and challenging behaviour, I need to help them see that 'how they defended' and 'how they survived' has developed a process that they can reliably call on. This behaviour has been shaped through the trauma exposure that has occurred over their journey and, in some cases, will still protect them.

When that child is confronted with a threat, a risk analysis process that they have fashioned involving visual and emotional responses activates within seconds. In some cases, threats seen by the child have not been identified by the adult; the accompanying adults (carers, teachers, support workers) don't register the environmental change, and so are left bewildered by the reaction of the child who then deals with the risk appraised. This is why some children will hit, run, shout or swear and adults are left behind. The child, well, they are just doing what all of us would do if we saw a threat – acting in the way we need to in order to be safe and secure.

> An 11-year-old told me how she was in fear of going to school and coming back to her foster carers. It was not the school or the home that was the difficulty; it was the journey, which she would make on foot. Her fear was that her birth father might be looking for her and he might try and take her away. That her birth father would be waiting after school and try and hurt her again. This young girl had already experienced four years in care and had not seen her birth family since; she was in a secure and loving placement, but her unresolved residual fears were dominant in those moments, and as such, she was most vulnerable. On one of the sessions with me, she explained that she saw her father in a car by the school and she had 'run for her life'.
>
> The sad thing in this case was that no one had told the girl that her father had died two years previously. It was not an oversight, but a purposeful decision by the social services department. I was asked to carry out therapeutic life story work with her, and so it was decided that I would tell her about her father. When I told her about her his death, she became upset and then thoughtful about him. We went to his grave, and on the way back she said, 'I can go to school safe now; my fear won't be there any more as he cannot hurt me.' This residue of fear was resolved, and over a short period of time, her school engagement and her education performance improved as her preoccupation lowered.

How do we reach our very, very challenging young people? How do we make sense of why they do the things they do? Quite simply, it is to provide our children and young people with a systemic approach that encourages their carer and therapeutic workers to bear witness to their journey and their stories. In doing so we help them to understand the ghosts of the past, and together, help them to decide whether their monsters of the present are still useful or can be left behind.

I will use this term, 'ghosts of the past', a few times in this book, but if grief and loss is something we learn to live alongside, to accept what has happened and be able to leave it where it belongs, what we have done is to accept the past as the past, to no longer be defined by it, because we can understand it. Our monsters, the behaviours we developed to manage these defined ghosts, are no longer needed as we make sense of the ghosts, and so we are no longer overwhelmed by them.

As we grow, we learn how to keep ourselves safe. If we are fortunate to have parental figures to do this for us when we need them the most, we learn that when we can't keep our self safe, our carers can, and do. Children who have learned that adults cannot keep them safe learn to do this themselves to the best of their own ability. These children create ways in which they can manage the world, but this might look and/or feel very distressing, combative or challenging in its operation. At the heart of this distressing behaviour is the need every one of us has – the need to be safe.

Traumatized children (and adults) often exist in crises and try to survive each day rather than planning for their tomorrow. They often live in fear, but then they manage that fear by developing responses that may increase risks to decrease fear, to give meaning to the emotional turmoil within. When their internal world is so frightening, the external world is dull; to equate their internal drive they may engage in behaviour that replicates or diverts from their state of self. We see children self-harm, take drugs, become very aggressive and violent, have worrying sexualized behaviours or become vulnerable to those who exploit them – all of which culminates in immeasurable harm, but also confirms their view that they lack esteem, that they are indeed worthless, and that they are unlovable.

What we try and do is help children understand that you do not have to be led by your past, that your past can't be rewritten. It's happened. Once you can make sense of your past and the way it may control you, well, that's when you are freer to make decisions to live your present and shape your future.

Several children I have worked with have been multiplaced, and so, if a new professional attends the child, the immediate conclusion might be 'I have to move again!'

> I once worked with a 12-year-old boy several years ago. He had been placed in 27 different care settings, and was already awaiting his 28th. He understood that adults couldn't keep him safe, so he was masterful in keeping himself safe. When adults

tried and showed him love, he saw that as dangerous, so he must push that love away. He told me that he had been 'therapized' to death...this is not a negative comment on therapy, but rather a reality that he had been subject to many therapy interventions but none had had the desired impact, or for each attempt, he had simply survived them.

I was asked to work with him, and I said to him, 'I'm Richard, the judge has asked if I might be any help for you?' He looked at me and he said, 'Well, my name is Isaac, and you need to know one thing about me – I have a monster in me, and I like him.' If I had replied with one or more of the following questions – 'Isaac, what's your monster's name?', 'What do you like about your monster?', 'It must be hard for you to have a monster?', 'Do you find it hard to have a monster?' or 'How does this monster keep you safe?', I am reminding him of a therapy intervention process that many people use, but all have failed for him.

This therapy model is known widely as the PACE model (Playfulness, Acceptance, Curiosity and Empathy), a model of practice introduced by Dan Hughes (Golding and Hughes 2012). If you are not familiar, check out Dan's approach around Dyadic Developmental Psychotherapy and the PACE approach (Hughes and Golding 2024).

Isaac needed to do something different, an approach that might not be questions but reflections from the adult perspective. I responded to his statement by simply telling him my truth. I said, 'That's really interesting; I've got a monster in me too.' He looked at me and then he said, 'Well, what's your monster like? What does your monster do? Does your monster get you in trouble like my monster?' and suddenly I've got a very different relationship, a connection where he is setting the pace, the topic and the opportunity. He is PACEing me!!!

Ghosts and monsters can 'pop' in the back of our heads – some of us can manage that and others can't. Every single child and young person I've worked with – every single one – has had monsters and ghosts that exist in the world around them and within them. That isn't helpful for them because they use behaviours which, when presented, are countered by the carer in a defensive or critical way. Behaviours are learned communication, and for most of the children I have worked with, and continue to work with, their behaviour is the only voice they have that gets the attention they need.

I have never worked with a monster, but I have worked with hundreds of children and adults who have had the most monstrous things happen to them. Understanding the past of the children we are working with can support our approach and avoid counter-transference of the unwelcome, or confused transference from the hurt child. Unless we help to unravel the past, how can we progress the child to a safer future?

If I can help children understand that some of these threats and experiences that they were shaped by in their early years are no longer valid for them, that these experiences of enduring and/or witnessing abuse can be thought through, can be understood to be a part of their history but not the drivers of their present and future, then we can have recovery. As children understand that their current protective behaviours are no longer needed, we can encourage their immediate carers and those influencing them to forge new behaviours and healthier strategies for their future. I still get amazing emails and letters from children and carers who have journeyed with me and, through their carer and their own tenacity, have moved forward. We have children who have gone on to graduate from universities such as Oxford and Cambridge, who have become lawyers, teachers, therapists and artists, and a good few who have become social care workers.

What we need to understand is that we have children who have a history, and if we understand their history, we can then understand how they make sense of their world. We need to be consistent, predictable and repetitive in all the things that we do. By doing so, the child doesn't have to wonder what, but know. The better relationships we can develop with the child and those around them, the more likely we can attune to the task as a team around the child and have congruence in our practice. With a surety for the child that those around them are working together, they are more likely to accept you as, 'Well, maybe you are different', and carers might see and understand that behaviours that are intolerable, undesirable and sometimes unmanageable come from experiences that have shaped the child they care for.

If we can support all those around the child, if we can work with our child to make sense of the past, then maybe we can move forward with the child. When you do this activity remember to take the lead and encourage the child and the carer to follow; do not worry that you are talking about monsters, because children know what monsters are and can cope with this as a process...after all, we have Minecraft™, Halloween and Harry Potter!

For this activity, draw a monster on the wallpaper or on a piece of paper in the top-left corner. Then ask the child and the carer to do the same, placing their pictures directly under yours. Now ask the child and the carer to think of three different words that might describe this monster, but make sure that you do the first three. You might choose 'Controlling, dangerous and scary'. Then ask the child and carer to do the same. These words should be written next to the monster picture that each has drawn.

Once complete, ask both the child and the carer if they have a monster in them – be sure to be the first one to say, 'I have one'. Put 'Yes' next to the words describing the monster. Describe for the child and the carer what your monster does – mine, for instance, gets sulky and can be moody. Your monster might be a shouty, angry, hitting or running monster. Once described, write each presentation next to the 'Yes'.

As this is completed, reflect on your journey of the monster and think about what happens to the people around you when you lose your internal control and the monster says hello. I would then write on my line of description, 'People back off, they step back', and then I would ask what happens when the child and the carer lose their sense of self, and we place that on the list. Finally, work through the list and then think how we feel when the monster goes back inside – this could be feelings of acceptance, shame, guilt and exhaustion.

Road rage is an example. When someone does something that makes you scared, you have lost your internal control. Even when the aggressive driver has gone ahead, you may still need time to right yourself, so you shout at them, gestate at them or swear so you start to feel better – the motorist who caused this has long gone, but your need to feel right needs to be aired.

Monsters are there to attack others, but also to protect us. We use what we know to keep ourselves safe. For children who have had monstrous things done to them, the need to be safe may be exhibited in very unsafe ways. A child may need to focus on the person who is dangerous and the dangerous person's needs rather than their own. A child may need to align themselves to the other (threat), to focus entirely on that person and attune to their needs and wants. The impact of this may lead to an inability to attune to their self, their own presentation or to understand their own needs. In a placement, the child will be trying to work out what the needs of the other person are, and align themselves with these – they are shaped or may attempt to shape their environment. The message is that we all get angry, but we need to 'master' and 'tame' our monsters. To do this, we need to be able to name our monsters, name our feelings about them and learn how to contain them.

Ghosts can also be used. The notion of ghosts as trauma has long been connected – I see trauma as the unresolved residuals of the past (the scary ghosts) and memories as resolved residuals of the past (the passive ghosts). As an example, the death of my brother was traumatic, and remains that way, but I have resolved the loss, and when I think about him, I think fondly of him and of my memory of his life – it is more manageable than that of when and how he died.

For older children, you could just talk about the concept of a ghost, something that is not quite there – you can see it in the corner of your eye, but it has an impact when it visits, and with unresolved residuals, it can hurt and be painful; it might mean that we have to call on our own reserves to protect ourselves and others.

The Australian Childhood Foundation describes trauma as the residual left after the event (Thomas 2019). I believe that this is a good definition, but I would change the concept that trauma is the residual left after, as it is not the wholesale residual, but the unresolved residuals that occupy our hearts, our heads and our souls. Resolved residuals are signs of a healthy processing of loss and grief, so that the memory is there, accepted, understood and part of who we are. It is the unresolved experiences of trauma, the unresolved emotions, the unresolved physiological and psychological residue that haunts and plays against our present and our future.

Trauma is the consequence of an event. Pain is the reality of the unresolved residual, whereas the resolved residual is accepted loss. Most of us who have suffered loss, in time we learn to live alongside the grief, and acknowledge the pain, emptiness and the impossibility of rewriting the past, and so loss is forever. The unresolved residuals are not understood; they hold power and have the effect of emerging in our conscious when least wanted, ghost-like and often more frightening than when the original experience first took place. The work required is to make sense of the unresolved residuals that the child is carrying. Many children and young people are defined by their past, and this prevents their present and future from shaping healthily.

To support children to understand the ghosts of their past, we can help tame the monsters of the now. In doing this, we, the child and the adults involved are conscious that the past is not able to be rewritten and should not continue to write our future. The past is the past, able to help us make sense; the present is the present, which, when reflecting, supports the questions of how we got where we are; and the future, well, our future should depend on the choices we make and the opportunities that we, when free, can make. I am not particularly religious, but a text from the Christian Bible – 'and you will know the truth, and the truth will set you free' – seems applicable here – truth will release the bonds of the past.

18

The Behaviour Tree

Understanding our past and how that past defines our present is key to recovery. Perry states that trauma recovery requires relationship, and that the best approach is love (Perry and Winfrey 2021). I agree, but in order to be loving, one must be loved. If we are faced with an angry, hurt, confused and defensive child, we feel under attack, threatened, undermined and disrespected. The child may see this very differently; they may see the behaviour as safe, distancing and secure. We need to understand our children and what they have experienced and how this has shaped their world – we are what we were, and until we make sense of that, to consider a different narrative, we will continue to reflect this experience of the past as a script of our future journey.

Once understood, we can move forward with freedom and hope. Using the behaviour tree is a good way for others (including carers and teachers) to understand what a child has experienced, to see the history (roots); it helps make sense of the behaviours, feelings and emotions (leaves), that they have a place and a space, they project us and protect who we are.

On a piece of paper or wallpaper, draw 12 tree leaves on the top half – these leaves need to be big enough for you to write a few words in. Reflect on a child you are working or have worked with, caring or have cared for, teaching or have taught, are supporting or have supported. Then, fill in the leaves by writing in each one behaviour or emotions that you see from the child (the illustration below should help you to complete the task).

For ease, I have put lots of my children's stories together, and as an example, I would identify behaviour such as 'angry', 'sexual behaving', 'self-harms', 'caring', 'defiant', 'not able to trust', 'night terrors', 'strategic' and 'controlling'. I would then consider emotions on show, and this might include 'anxious', 'shame' and 'emotionally dysregulated'. You might have something like this:

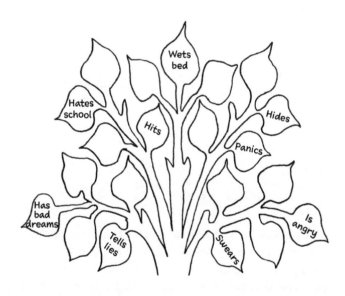

Have a go. Once done, look at the more challenging behaviours, and consider what this looks like in practical terms, and note these in the leaves or branches. Finally, do the same with the emotions leaves so that you can connect what you have written to the actions on show. Beverly James (1989) suggests that 'All behaviour is communication'. So what do you think the children you care for, or work for, are saying to you through their presenting behaviour and emotions? Consider the reasons for the behaviour and what lies beneath, and reflect on the emotions and how they have formed since you have known the child.

On the piece of paper, leave a gap underneath the leaves and then draw around 12 tree roots; each of the roots should cross over others, as if they are the real roots of a tree. Once done, think about the child you have in mind and on each root identify a past experience the child has lived through and what you know about the family of origin. With the same case example, I might identify the following roots: 'sexual abuse', 'domestic violence', 'birth mum with learning challenges', 'cultural trauma', 'drugs and alcohol challenges', 'grief' and 'death of older sibling'.

Have a go at detailing the history of the child and what they have lived through. Once completed, reflect on the roots and how they may have impacted on the child. When looking at the roots, can you see whether the child you care for, or work for, believes they are worthy, loveable, protected, loved, cared for and safe? Your roots might look like this:

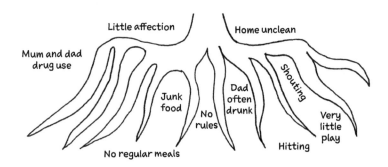

Do they, when you see the tree roots and the behaviours in the leaves, seem that they are living in a world where they feel belonging, where they have a place, where they have a space and where they feel wanted? Or does it seem that the child has learned that they are unimportant, unprotected and unlovable, and that the adults around them are unsafe, that they do not have a place or space or even belong in the world they occupy?

> As one child said to me, 'I was born into this; it was not my making.'

Through this process, we can learn how the child gets their needs met (to keep them safe) or how they learn that their needs are unmet (which means they are unsafe). It might be that you've learned to be in control. It gives you a sense of purpose, and being out of control is too scary. Do you see how this works? Now we'll see how you feel about this later, but for me, that's what I need to understand for my children.

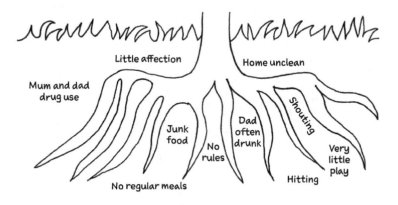

On the piece of paper, draw a green line that sits on top of the roots – this is the grass at the base of the soon-to-be-drawn trunk. This line covers up the roots and, in a way, covers up the causal factors – the roots of the behaviour identified in the leaves. Some of you might have thought long and hard about the roots but realize how little you know. Many of the carers I work with have not been told in detail the history of their child they are caring for, and the same is often the case for schools, too.

Next, draw a tree trunk to link the roots to the tree leaves, and now you have a behaviour tree. We are all of us what we were, and our stories define us. We also have a psychodynamic picture of what lies beneath – look at the final tree you have drawn and see if you can connect some of the behaviours to some of the history. As a communication exercise, I have done this directly with children, and in doing so, we have been able to talk about the past events of their lives and the way they manage these. To explain this in a picture of life is really helpful, and a number of carers who have completed trees with me have said, 'It's not me, it's not that they don't like me, you can see why he behaves the way he does. I think I might have done the same things too.'

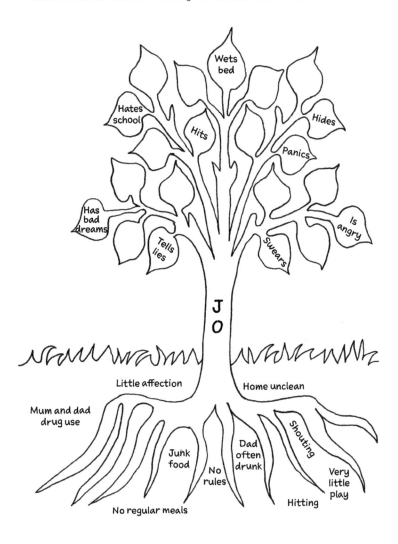

All the children you work with, and I work with, are incredibly intelligent. You may not see it, but if you imagine a child who is living in fear, they must be so clever to be able to survive that fear. The trouble is that all that intelligence is used in the wrong space. What we know about the work we do with children is that, as we start to release that fear and it starts to not dominate them any more, they then fly, they then become extremely able.

I had a child I worked with about four years ago. She had been terribly hurt by both parents, and as a result, both parents received prison sentences. The injuries she received resulted in her being admitted to hospital for treatment, and while in hospital they found she had a life-threatening illness. So she had all her emergency treatment as an inpatient. She managed to get through all that, and then I was asked to work with her about the abuse and the impact of the loss of her parents, but also, I worked with her because she had a distrust of the adults who got too close. In short, her behaviour reflected her insecurity.

By working through the behaviour tree, she and her family were able to identify why she found the concept of trust so challenging. As we started to make sense of what was hers and what wasn't, she began to have a greater sense of efficacy and dealt with shame that was not hers to bear. Just a few months ago, I was emailed by her wonderful carers to be told, 'Just thought I'd let you know, Richard, our daughter has just started reading Law at university.' This young person, angry at her 'self', angry at the world just four years earlier, had freed herself from the authority of her past to shape her own future! The tree was the start.

I am lucky that I still work directly with children.

A few years ago I worked with a young person who was out of school. He was very angry at the world. He was very much at a loss as he was not with his mum and dad. He lived in a foster family he didn't want to be in. He found it hard to be told what he had to do and so became very angry towards his carers, particularly the female carer. He wanted to emulate the parents' behaviours and attitudes in any way he could, to keep them alive in his head.

When I met him, the first time, no way would those around him see that he would be able to engage as he had. No way would people have believed that he could endure thinking about what had happened to him in his past and how it affected him in the present.

He had been out of school for several years, and yet, within six months of working together, he restarted at school and is now planning to attend university to study History and Politics! Not where many people around him thought of at the time, where those caring and making decisions for him were predicting prison and long-term engagement with support services.

Bronfenbrenner (Brendtro and Ness 1983) reminds us that every child needs an adult insanely crazy about them. This insanity of love and care is a prerequisite of carers that is needed to provide for children in care. As the carer builds relationships with the children they care for, so the risk of potential hurt increases for the child as they may expect to be let down, turned away or the placement fail. To test this, the behaviour of the child may reflect the risk they experience and the memories they hold – 'Can you still cope with me? Can you still hold me? Can you still love me if I do this, if you see what I am really like?' Those of us that have worked closely with hurt children know that they will hurt the ones they love in the hope that those are the people who can hold them safe.

Of course, it is not just the insanity that carers need. According to Bronfenbrenner, it is finding ways to slow the thought processes down and allow reflection and comprehension (Brendtro and Ness 1983). Many children are diagnosed with a range of different labels, be this ADHD, Asperger's, autism and many more; with traumatized children, the behaviour has developed from early life trauma and developing skills to keep safe. The problem is that those memories of trauma, often unable to be verbalized, lie in the hippocampus unresolved. They lie until awoken, by a word, a feeling, a noise, something seen or smelled. Once awake, the memory takes them right back to the original trauma causing fear, all-consuming pain, and can overwhelm and send to the rescue the behaviours associated with the defence they know best works.

Stephen King, in his book *Wizard and Glass*, writes

so do we pass the ghosts that haunt us later in our lives, they sit undramatically by the roadside like poor beggars, and we see them only from the corner of our eyes, if we see them at all. The idea that the have been wating for us rarely if ever crosses our minds. Yet they do wait, and when we have passed, they gather up their bundles of memory and fall in behind, treading in our footsteps and catching up, little by little. (King 1997, p.361)

The concept of memories catching up with us is real. For many of the children I have worked with, they have to be busy, they have to be moving and doing, and they find it hard to sit still for a few moments. Meerkats are often the animal we identify to describe hypervigilant and on-guard children, not able to relax as the threats are not far away. The danger is, of course, internal rather than external; it is the guard against the recalling of past events. If you slow down, if you take time to think or not to think, the memory starts to not only catch up, but to envelop. The memory is painful and aggressive, and when it is fully exposed, becomes the pain of the unresolved residual being held and carried.

> As one 20-year-old told me, 'These memories catch me up, and when they get me, it feels like a forceful hit in the back of my head. If I don't let them catch me, if I keep busy, I am safe.'

If you're someone who has been impacted by trauma through abuse by a parent figure and you are reading this, it will take you straight back to that memory, whether you wish it to or not. You can't forget this; it invades your present, and so impacts on your next thought. Some may shut this book; others might need to take a break; and others might be able to acknowledge the reality of what they carry.

To be busy is a great defence; to cause chaos and deflect is all about protecting the self.

> I remember, a few years ago, working with a child I thought was travelling well, but, as he was drawing pictures on the piece of paper we were working on, and I was busy talking in a very general way about his birth family, all of a sudden he became very angry and pushed the table we were working on to the floor. He left the room swearing about how he hated me and everyone.
>
> As I picked the table and its contents up, I noticed what he had been drawing – penises and angry faces. I had got so carried away with my agenda that I hadn't been as observant as I should have been. When he came back to the room, I apologized that I had not held the room safe, and he asked if I had seen his drawing. I nodded and he said, 'That was all I could see in my head, and nothing else was going in – it was horrible, it was my dad!'

Let me give you another worked example (a case constructed for this exercise, but based on a true scenario).

A girl, she was almost six and already in her seventh placement; things were not going well, and her carer was considering ending the placement. When learning the child's history, I found that she had been sexually abused from six months to three years old, and once this was discovered she was removed from her family and placed with foster carers she had never met.

Do you think that she was aware that she had been harmed sexually? She may only have understood that what had happened was normal, that a narrative given to her as this abuse was occurring may have told her that this was love, a special love, a love that was secret between her and her parents. The repeated commentary develops permission, acceptance and understanding that this 'love' that was happening to her was wonderful and special. This little girl, at age three, had behaviours she didn't understand, but knew how to do the things she had learned.

As her carers began to care for her, to provide routine, food, warmth and shelter, she felt loved and wanted to love them. This may be shown by touching, showing or acting in a way that was seen by the carers as sexual behaviour but meant by the child as love. The sad thing is that the behaviour was challenging, scary and had to be addressed, but if the carers told her, 'This is not acceptable', 'This is rude', 'You mustn't do this', she may hear her carers really saying, 'Love is not acceptable', 'Love is rude', 'You mustn't love here'. Sadly, the carers were confused by her behaviour as she struggled with this new environment, and things remained unsettled.

A few weeks into the placement, the carers decided to bring their grandchildren to the house, and at some point, the children were left alone and later found in a situation that was not appropriate. The carers were horrified, and this led to their own children refusing to allow the grandchildren to visit until this little girl had been removed.

On her second family placement, she found herself living with a little boy who knew exactly how to love like she did, and before long, they were both in a situation that was not appropriate. She was blamed for this as the boy had not shown any of this behaviour until she came to live with him. A few short days into the placement, she was moved again. By the time she got to her seventh placement, she had reached the conclusion that this adult worrying behaviour she had was very powerful – it could break placements, cause adults to panic and she could have control of this.

In her seventh placement, she was regarded as a child with unsafe behaviour towards others, unable to live with other children, and also in need of a full-time carer who was not employed. She was placed with a single female carer. Things went well for a while, as both she and her carer performed their dances of attachment (where social care workers often use the concepts of a 'Honeymoon period'). Around two months into the placement, the carer decided that the child was settled enough, and she invited her friend for tea, a new addition to the household for just a few moments. The little girl, now six, saw this new addition as a threat, a threat she needed to manage, but what could she do about an adult? How could a little six-year-old get rid of this adult-sized threat?

She had, of course, the perfect behaviour. She started to try and touch them on their privates, she showed them her privates, she crawled over them and talked to them by using sexual language and sexual noises. How would you react? Would you feel nervous, attacked, compromised, embarrassed, angry? I would suggest that for most it would be 'How do I get out of here?'...and once you/I/they left, the child would feel safe and had her carer, once more, to herself. The threat was removed and the protective outcome of the most worrying of behaviours reinforced her capacity to be this way when adults were present.

The child learned that this sexual behaviour was not something done to feel sexy, to be an invitation for any kind of sexual response. It was not something dangerous, naughty, exciting or attention-seeking for the child, but simply an absolute perfect way to be safe.

Remember in earlier chapters of this book – if it works and if it works then it becomes behaviour? In this girl's situation, it was her 'go-to', that action she had that she could depend on. When you know that adults can be unsafe, you learn how to be safe – and that may be to comply, defy, shut down or be creative, and our clever children are very creative. For the adult who has been the subject of the behaviour, it is seen as sexual behaviour that is dangerous, unsafe or abusive, and that others need to be protected from.

With this wonderful child in mind, I was and still am convinced that if an adult reciprocated these types of behaviours and became sexual in response, the child involved would have been shocked, stunned and internal panic would lead to her overwhelmingly disconnecting from those around her. Dr Bessel van der Kolk (2015) reminds us that many traumatized children noted that when they were under stress, and they could not control the situation, they could make themselves 'disappear'.

If we go back to the behaviour tree, these challenging behaviours that we see are not about the child and their need to act badly, but rather their need to act safely! You will find the same in situations where children have endured domestic abuse and other chaotic and dangerous environments. It is important to understand that behaviour as we see it is not necessarily what is happening. Beverly James (1989) reminds us that all behaviour is communication – the need for us to understand the root cause that has led to the communication they are acting out is essential, and sadly, the behaviour is a consequence of when the roots of the behaviour go unnoticed.

What do we do about this, though? Are these behaviours stuck? Thankfully, they are not. We all have coping strategies, but if these are called on again and again and again, the strategy is no longer a strategy, but a behaviour. If I have learned that the only way I can keep myself safe is to do what other people think is unsafe, then I do what is unsafe for them and ultimately safe for me.

Let us look at an amalgamation of older children's stories.

Here is the story of a 10-year-old girl. She did her behaviour tree and it was a very honest reflection of her presentation. It had 'swearing', 'shouting', 'hitting' and 'angry' actions along-side 'kind', 'engaging' and 'achieving' behaviour. We then did her roots, what she had experienced when she was in the care of her birth family. In the roots, she wrote 'violence', 'anger', 'drugs', 'alcohol', 'separation', 'neglect' and 'sexual hurt'. Once completed, I asked her if she could see any links between her past and present. She could, but she also felt that her past was still present, that the dangers, the people who were harmful to her, were still there. She confirmed that they were still a risk, and as such she had to be 'on guard' – to look out for danger, such as her mother finding her and taking her away.

I have this rule of thumb, well, several rules of thumbs and fingers really, but this one is about child development: seven-year-olds are thinking, 'Who am I?'; 11-year-olds 'Who am I and who are you?' and 13-year-olds 'Who am I and who the hell are you?'

This almost 11-year-old was, like many care-experienced children, way ahead of her years in survival terms and way behind in her emotional wellbeing. She was very skilled at pushing her carer away, demanding for her to put her back with her birth mother and rejecting the care she had experienced. She was sure that her mother would get her in the end and was exhausted waiting for the day, even though this would have been the last thing she wanted.

This child's carer was amazing, and she asked the child whether she would put new roots on her tree as they had spent so much time together and they had shared love, care, fun and happiness. For a moment the child considered this, and then said, 'No'. She explained that her tree was her tree and that the roots were not part of her foster home. The carer was visibly upset, but the child drew a leaf and put the word 'callous' on it. She informed her carer that she was 'not callous any more, though, am I?' and the leaf she had drawn was disconnected to the tree as the child said this 'behaviour had fallen away'. The carer responded by writing other behaviour on the leaves, and explained, 'You don't do many things that you used to do. I am sure some of these attached with your tree will fall away as we continue to work with Richard.'

The best thing on completing the tree was where the carer identified that as the difficult leaves fell to the ground it left space for new leaves, such as 'great at being a daughter', 'funny and silly in a good way'. In other words, therapeutically healing as the trauma of the past and the behaviour of the present reasons were no longer required, understanding the past trauma and responses no longer defensive, her new thinking had negated the old.

While we are in this space, it might be worth considering the chaos/ chaos concept that I developed when helping carers to make sense of the child's behaviour when they seem to reject the care they receive. When children are living in a chaotic space, say, with family, but there are considerable concerns for the way the child's needs are unmet, this might be as a result of neglect, emotional harm, domestic violence, sexual harm or/and physical harm that becomes the child's day-to-day experience. A referral initiates an investigation by social workers, and this follows potential actions of support, child protection measures, family support and other contributions within the community and wider family, but sadly, despite all this, change does not always occur, and concerns lead to the removal of the child. The child is removed to a 'healthy' family where there is more potential for the child's needs to be addressed, met and their wellbeing secured.

What has happened in this scenario mirrors much of what we see in a protective approach – the child has been removed from what we see as chaos and danger, and placed in a healthy, routine-based environment of care and attention. For the child, though? Have they moved from chaos to stability, or have they been removed from what they know and been placed in, what to them may well be the chaos of the unknown?

The child has been removed from their 'known', their already honed survival and vigilance routine; from the look of mum and the gait of dad, they know when to hide, when to endure and when to run, when to be quiet, when to eat, when to respond and when not to. In a new family, one they have no knowledge of, they may believe that, like all adults they have experience of, the new family harbour dangers, threats and the unpredictability of the unknown, and they find themselves in a place where they know nothing.

Many of those involved in the foster care/out of home care space talk of the first weeks of care as a 'Honeymoon period'. There is no such thing; there is just a cessation of behaviour as both the new carers and the child are dancing a new dance of attachment, to try and assess both the dangers and the opportunities. For the children I often work with, once this is done, they need to test their theories, and so they begin to push. This period of scoping the threats of the new environment may be watchful, careful and non-confrontational, until the threats and opportunities are being probed.

As the child becomes more aware, they need to test their

assessments and push; they are expecting responses that they are used to, and when this doesn't happen, they need to understand why. In many cases, when the child may behave in a negative way, they might be surprised that they have not been hit or punished, as they experienced in their family home. This confusion may lead to them asking their carer, 'Why didn't you hit me? This is what happens at home.' The carer may respond by stating that 'No one is allowed to hit anyone in this placement' or 'Hitting children is wrong' or 'We don't do that!'

Conventional wisdom might suggest that the child, on hearing that they are not going to be hit, may feel relief, that they might feel safe, but the opposite happens. If you don't hit, then what do you do? Where is the boundary? How do they know when they have gone too far? This can become overwhelming for the child; it may feel chaotic and the environment unpredictable, but to be safe, they have to know where the punishment line is drawn.

These children need to see the boundary, to know where it is, and the only way they can feel safe is knowing the boundary is strong and containing. Without clarity, the child may need to push and push, to understand where the barrier is. Sadly, the pushing for the child in this scenario isn't always understood, and if the behaviour continues, then the carer and the family will start to question if the placement is right. This starts to undermine the carer's authority and the child's safety, and eventually, if not addressed, the collapse of placement is inevitable.

For me, in therapeutic life story work, I experience this chaos/chaos theory, and in information gathering see that so many placements break down due to the unknown moving into the unknown. Some of these placements would not have disrupted if more had been done to address this concept. Indeed, in our work we talk about these breakdowns and demystify the chaos, and hopefully become more in tune with the known child and the known carer.

19

The Animal Game

The animal game is a really good way of thinking about ourselves and the way we see and are seen by others. For some children, when asked to think about themselves, or to comment on their thoughts, they cannot; the reason may be that it is too big a risk for them. The animal game has been used by many therapeutic professionals, but here is a way that you might find helpful, and I have had some great outcomes.

Mum
Tiger

Dad
Dog

Think of animals that represent you and those you might be working with.

I was working with a 13-year-old boy and his carer. There were challenges for both in their relationship, mainly around control.

I asked the young person to think of an animal that represented me, one that represented his carer and one for himself, to write the animals down but not to show anyone. I then asked the carer to do the same and I completed my list of three.

Once done, I asked who wanted to reveal first, and the boy was very keen to go first. For me he had decided I was most like a sloth! I have never been called a sloth before, and I was curious. I explained that I am often likened to a polar bear, or a grizzly bear, due to my size, my beard etc., but not a sloth. I asked and he explained that I never react to anything that people say in a shocked or negative way, and that I just continue calmly; he said I was 'slow'. 'Slow' is not a description I would use, but again, I was interested, and he informed me that he didn't feel rushed, and that we talked about all the difficult things in a way that gave him a chance to work things out. I asked him whether it was good to be a sloth and he assured me it was – I quite liked being a sloth.

His foster carer was next, and she was worried that the things he might say would be hurtful, insulting or mean, but he said that she was a deer. She was pleased and remarked that she feared he would be nasty and asked him why she felt he was a deer. He looked at me and then turned to her and said, 'You're like Bambi. At the slightest sign of trouble, you run away.' She was shocked by this, but then, after thinking it through, she said he was right. That when he got very angry, she got scared and so left the home and sat in her car for 30 minutes, waiting for him to calm down. He said that when she did that, he got even more scared and angry and that he needed her to be with him so that she could keep him safe. He wanted her to be more like an elephant, strong and safe.

Another child I worked with had lived in his birth family where violence was a constant experience. The child found it very hard to speak about it. On one occasion he mentioned that his mother loved him and the other children, but that she didn't have the power to keep him and them safe. I got the animals out and asked him to assign an animal to each person in his birth family. Once done, we got some Jenga® blocks out and made a square enclosure (pen) and housed each of the animals in the animal pen.

His father was a tiger, his mother a rabbit, his two sisters were guinea pigs and he was a dog. I then said that it must have been very hard for all these animals to live in the same space, and queried what might happen if the tiger became angry? He then, with no hesitation, played out the hurt, the fear, the behaviour of all in his family to the violence. He was able to think about this and start to make sense of it. It is a great way for children to speak about very difficult experiences, and very soon the animals were pushed to one side.

I have used this process with children who have been bullied at school, feel apart and not included. I have used the animals to talk about feelings, hopes, fears and challenging issues such as being hurt, neglected and other difficult life events such as loss, separation and critical conversations.

Think of what animal you are most like, and then why that particular animal. Now think of the people you are with – what animals would they be? How do we live alongside each other? What behaviours do we see? How do we deal with these? How do we get along?

20

Cause and Effect Thinking

Cause and effect thinking supports every child and young person to thrive and survive. Most children understand that if they do something, there will be certain consequences. I remember with my own children when they were very young the phrase we used regularly was 'Remember, for every action there is a reaction', and we would, my wife and I, provide ongoing commentary to help bed that in their decision-making. We now see this still guiding their behaviour and actions in their adult life. When I work with children and young people, it is not the hurt child I am trying to support but, more importantly, the child as an emerging adult.

It is this focus that will have the greatest outcome, to try and break the cycles of intergenerational trauma and generational engagement with social care. So many of the children I meet with in their current generation have parents and grandparents who were also seeing social workers in their childhood years. Our aim should be that this current generation is the last of our clients, and as adults, they become the parents/carers of a new generation of confident, loving and loved children.

The majority of children I meet are extremely clever, but these skills are often concentrated on survival, of attuning to the threats and the potential hurts that they are familiar with rather than the opportunities and hopes that we need to thrive. It is for this that the concepts of consistency, predictability and repetition are essential for the wellbeing of traumatized and attachment-challenged children.

However, there is a way in which we can assist children to understand the concepts of action and reaction – by introducing 'cause and effect thinking', a process that encourages children to not only understand the concept of cause and effect, but also to add conscious thought-through decision-making once understood.

Games allow for this to mature as we journey through childhood, whether noughts and crosses (tic-tac-toe) or Ludo, to most card games such as UNO!™, and then to the clearest 'cause and effect thinking' game of all, chess. When I am working with very angry children, who are often quick to lose their internal control, introducing games that require strategy become rehearsals for life.

These games are more and more lost to our early childhood as solitary game play and online games become the norm. A few years ago I was often asked to undertake court assessments to consider what therapy may assist the child who was of concern. The outcomes of these assessments were mainly to recommend family members playing games, and most of that play should be strategic. We developed play as an intervention and not as a therapy, a chance to reintroduce the opportunity of attunement, a crucial ingredient to the ideal attachment recipe.

An example of this happened when I was working with a family where the foster carers were struggling with the behaviour of the four children they were caring for. We attempted to improve relationships by counselling, family therapy and activity-based emotion work, but to little avail. I decided that we should try and play some games. We considered lots of different games, but Monopoly® won the day. As we set the game up, the carers announced that they had to go and sort their car out. I asked them not to go but to join in, and they were unhappy about this. Thankfully, though, they agreed to stay and join in.

As the game progressed, the alliances, the debating, arguing and resolving unfolded, and as it did, the foster carers were drawn more and more into the play. There was laughter, smiling, eye contact, touch, rocking and singing, the interplay of which created weaving of attachment. The family agreed that they should have one play date a week, and that all had to do their best to be there. Over the months, the family grew closer together, and my engagement and that of others fell away.

In my trauma work with children, I introduce noughts and crosses, and as we play, we discuss the process of decision-making – what did they do? What can I do? What might they do next? How will that affect me? We move on from that to games such as UNO!™ or Jenga® using the same questions, and as we continue, we start to think about real-life situations at school, at home, or when with friends.

The ultimate game is chess, and for my eight-year olds and older, we learn to play this and work out that in some games of chess we sacrifice pieces, we defend pieces, we attack and we can submit. As we play, we strategize, we think of moves and assume our opponent's moves. Sometimes we are right and sometimes we are wrong – but without cause and effect thinking, when we are wrong, we become frustrated and often the board is thrown in the air and disappointment becomes overwhelming. In many cases this leads to frustration, anger and challenge. With cause and effect thinking, when we are wrong, we can take a deep breath and think it through; we can re-strategize and find a new way to win, or at best, not lose.

In practice, what we see in cause and effect thinking might be the child who needs consistency, predictability and repetition. An example of this can be found when a child unsure of school will plan their day at school the night before. They work out that Miss Thomas will be in class when they get there, and their teaching assistant (TA) Miss Crowther will have her reassuring smile. They will have maths and then – therefore the child has rehearsed the day.

When the child gets to school the next day, they don't see Miss Thomas, but there is a new teacher called Mrs Desroches, but they don't know this teacher well. Panic might ensue. This is not what they expected, and can the new teacher keep them safe and do the things that Miss Thomas does? They don't see Miss Crowther either, and start to feel unsafe, and become overwhelmed. Their only means of safety is to get out of the classroom, and there begins the challenge to remain. The change in teacher and feeling vulnerable and unsafe creates insecurity and they cannot re-think or re-strategize.

Cause and effect thinking will help a child to not only strategize when things are attempted, but also be able to re-strategize when things don't go the way that they had hoped.

Chess and other games are not the only way to achieve this skill, however. I would like to introduce to you sequency work that really gets results and is easy to do, and that can support the building blocks to competency. I have worked with families where children struggle with their emotions and, over a few weeks, become trapped in a behavioural cycle where the behaviour was dealt with by punishment but the punishments served to reinforce the poor behaviour.

Let's look at a worked example of many children into one case study.

> When Jessica got angry, because she got called names at school, she didn't know how to deal with this. If she got angry and shouted or hit people, she would get into trouble. She might get embarrassed or feel shamed, but she couldn't show this, so she sucked in all the hurt, the rage and shame, and stored it in her head. After a whole day of this, she was full of feelings that she could not show and arrived home fit to burst. It took just a 'Hello' from her carer and the dam burst and the hurt, anger and shame were projected out and directed at the carer. Although this is similar to Melanie Klein's transference and counter-transference theory (1952), it is really cause and effect thinking, as the carer didn't have to counter-transfer back to be swept up in the behaviour cycle.
>
> To map out Jessica's behaviour cycle, you need her and her carer to be in a calm space – and then explain that you are trying to make sense of the behaviour presented. It is important that the child is not feeling told off. With this young person, I asked her and her carer to draw a flowchart that would, when followed, help them make cheese on toast. What would your first action be? Check for ingredients? Turn the grill on? Jessica and her carer did this flowchart, with actions, questions and outcomes. As we attempted to follow the directions, we didn't get past the third step before we could go no further.

Give this a go and you will see how many steps you miss or assume when we are doing tasks practically, without thinking.

It is a bit like unconscious/conscious concepts – the steps of enlightenment. If we don't know we don't know something, ignorance is bliss. When we then realize that we don't know something that we should know, it gets awkward. So we learn what we don't know and move to the next level of knowing that we know something. If, over time, we get more and more confident, we might get to the point that we don't need to know what we know. An easier way of thinking about this is when we learn to drive.

As a child, I don't need to know how to drive because I am not allowed to drive – I am unconsciously unconscious. At 17, I am allowed to drive, but I don't know how to – I am consciously unconscious. I then learn to drive and I know how to drive – I am consciously conscious. After a few years of knowing how to drive, I no longer think about what I am doing, I just do it – I am unconsciously conscious. My aim for Jessica is to help her to be consciously conscious, aware of what she needs to be aware of and thinking through before she acts – to mirror, signal and manoeuvre, for example.

I drew Jessica's behaviour cycle from the moment that she left school and started as she arrived home, full of anger, hurt and shame. I asked her how she felt after a bad day and what happened when she got home from school. She told me that she slammed the front door so that her carer (mum) knew she was not okay. Then she got angry with her carer for sending her to school. Jessica told me that she shouted loudly and would not listen to her carer, and then got even more angry as she began to scream.

She then told me that she sang loudly and in her carer's face. Her carer said that she found this the most difficult, and although she knew it was not a good idea, she shouted at Jessica and eventually sent her to her bedroom. Here, Jessica became very angry at herself; she began to hate herself, and this is where she got really scared. I asked her how she got out of this, and she responded by saying that she was very sorry that everyone was unhappy and tried to find a way to tell her carer what was wrong and when she could do this, she felt better.

This cycle was becoming an established behaviour, and as such, the carer was pre-empting the cycle by becoming angry with Jessica much earlier than warranted. We talked about how we might try and do something different. The carer thought about things she could do differently, and we looked at the cause and effect of the cycle. In just a few moments, Jessica chose a colour and made a mark on the picture we had done.

Jessica explained that when she got home and was angry, if her carer didn't get angry with her, but remained calm and reminded her that she could talk to her about what was wrong, then she could tell her carer what was wrong, who she was angry at; the flowchart helped her to see that the shouting had the consequence of being sent to her room.

Once the flowchart was complete, we made several copies and put them around the foster home, so that they were easy to see. We placed them in the kitchen, hallway, bedroom and bathroom areas. These copies were not for Jessica; if they were, they would be ripped down almost immediately. They were for Jessica's carer, so that she could walk to the flowchart as Jessica verbally attacked, and read it calmly aloud. This provides room for the carer to regulate and then to respond more calmly to Jessica's distress…it works and it separates out the hurt and the behaviour.

Over time, Jessica subsequently learned to interrupt the escalation cycle by choosing to tell her carer what had happened when she was upset. Now, when she feels angry, Jessica elects to talk to her carer, and this is an opportunity to talk about and seek comfort and calming, thus avoiding the old behaviour cycle of anger, shame and frustration. I refer to it as cause and effect thinking because, every now and again, Jessica may choose or have a need for confrontation, but the difference is, she is deciding whether to or not.

Try this for all agreements where the adult takes responsibility – to reflect, to regulate, and then to respond – the secret of parenting, really! I have completed these exercises many times with children and they have had success.

One wonderful young person was purposely making her adoptive mum late for work in the mornings as she didn't want to go to school. We drew clocks and times when her mother needed to be ready as part of the flowchart – if the child and her carer were ready, they would reward each other by having a hot chocolate drink, which had been gently simmering on the cooker. This child went further. A few weeks later she used a similar technique to help her get to the classroom in a calm state. Each morning, at school but before class, she would make sure everything was ready, and if it was, she and her teaching assistant would share a flask of hot chocolate (made by the child at home) before going into the maelstrom of the class.

21

What 'SAFE' Means, and Other Acrostics

This activity brings about discussions with uncomfortable topics and themes for individual children, and can be used for children of all ages. Use wallpaper or a large piece of paper.

What is the child's understanding of 'unsafe'? Write the word 'UNSAFE' in giant letters on a large piece of paper. What does this word mean to the child? Each word becomes a chance for narrative, and using each letter as the first letter of a word connected with UNSAFE has another opportunity for a story. For example, what does it look and feel like when you are nervous, or scared and not in control? What other things make you scared?

Using acrostics can be a useful tool as it allows the word itself to be considered, but also invites descriptions, vocabulary and reflection. Once the word 'UNSAFE' is completed, think of other words, such as 'SAFE', 'SCHOOL' and 'FAMILY'.

Here is an example of how a child might complete the acrostics. This child was 14 at the time. What was the child's understanding of 'UNSAFE' and 'SAFE'?

U = Unsure

    N = Nervous
    S = Scared
    A = Afraid
    F = Frightened
    E = Excited

S = Secure

A = Attached
F = Friend and family safe
E = Eye-catched (meaning, to be safe by others keeping an eye on me)

It is not only the words 'safe' and 'unsafe' that work. You may have a child struggling with the concept of friends – 'FRIEND': Faithful, Reliable, Including me, Exciting, Nice and Dependable. Or not just acrostics, you could use a word like 'vulnerable'. When I work with children who are at risk of exploitation, what does that look and feel like? In utilizing acrostics, children share their experiences of the word and how they might act or struggle with the story behind the word. By spending time just considering what it takes to be safe, and who in their world might help them to feel safe, can lead to safer behaviour.

> As one child said to her carer, 'Your job is to keep me safe. Your job is to keep me forever. Your job is to keep people safe around me. I don't have to do this on my own any more.'

As with acrostics you can just spell the word out and then think with the child what the word might mean to them and to those around them. Here is a worked example – again, an amalgamation of several cases.

> I was working with a 13-year-old child who was very vulnerable to other children at her school who were trying to get her to pose without clothes on and post the photos on social media. She thought it would be okay as they might like her more if she did what they said, and she worried they might reject her if she didn't. The hard part for her was that one of the girls trying to get her to do this was her best friend.
>
> We wrote out the word 'VULNERABLE' across her wallpaper and thought of all the words that we could link to it. We got to phrases – when she thought about it, she wrote 'vulnerable means being tricked' and another meaning was 'using me to get their fun'. She accepted that friends, especially best friends, don't do what these 'friends' had done, and that those she

had at first wanted to like were only trying to make her feel worthless.

You can also spend time thinking about words that might be used for their legal status, such as 'care', 'adoption', 'Special Guardianship Orders', 'Care Orders', 'Contact Agreements', and similar.

22

Think, Feel, Do

I think (brain): What am I thinking?
I feel (heart): How do I feel?
I do (hand): What am I doing/what do I do?

You can use a bear or a person stencil for this. Once copied out, ask the child to draw a heart in the chest area, a brain in the head area, and draw fingers and thumbs in the hands of the stencil.

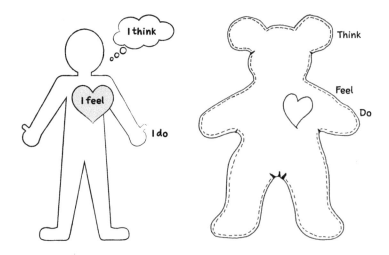

On the reverse side, you, or who you are working with, can write 'I feel' in the heart area, 'I think' in the head area, and finally 'I do' in the hands area.

If you can complete these stencils with the child or young person, then you can start to explore the thoughts, feelings and behaviours that are current to the conversation – say, about school. 'I think school is...', 'When I'm in my class I feel...', 'The best things I do at school are...'

If you do not wish to create a stencil, then, with the innovation of three social workers in Sydney, Australia – Amy Payne, Karen Vance and Natalia O'Keefe, we have the Think, Feel, Do Bear (TFD Bear).

These bears are proving extremely useful when working through emotions, thoughts and actions, and in Australia, the TFD Bear won an award, as an aid to support children impacted by the trauma of the recent bushfires. I use these bears or stencils in most of my work with children and young people. The bear is particularly useful as it is the same weight as a weighted blanket. It can have sensory fabric for the heart, hands and brain as well as a smell pouch for comfort.

If you were working through a child's reflection of their birth mother and her actions, you could explore their thoughts, feelings and actions by using the bear or a stencil. If you were working with a child who is quick to anger, the bear or stencil can be used to work through the anger event and seek understanding: 'I thought he wanted to hurt me. I felt scared, so I hit him first' – to another view, 'I think I should have sought help. I felt scared but also angry. Hitting him might be good but not afterwards, as I would be in trouble', to 'I think hitting him would be wrong. I need to get help to be safe. I feel angry and this isn't okay. I will walk away and tell someone who can support me.'

Finally, you could just use the bear or stencil and ask the child how they are coping with the notion of 'safe'. By using the 'people'-shaped stencil, we can help children identify safe and unsafe touch, safe and unsafe thoughts, and safe and unsafe feelings. Once established, we can think what is safe, how to stay safe and how to be safe with others.

With the stencil drawn by you on a piece of paper, identify an event that recently happened in your world...then follow the process. Detail the event and what happened as a result of the event to a friend, partner or colleague. Discuss this and write down some of your actions and new reflected actions by identifying what you originally thought, what you now think, what you originally felt, and what you now feel, and finally, what you originally did and what you would do differently.

23

The Wall

The wall is one of my most favourite activities to do with children and young people in care, as well as with care providers and support workers. It is widely used in foster care training, and its original thinkers are hard to identify, but I have used this approach for many years, and a brief internet search will provide a good explanation for its use with carers and potential adopters.

As with many of the activities and interventions I have identified in this book, the original idea has been worked on and shaped over years and hundreds of interventions to this approach, leading to the therapeutic life story work wall of development and understanding.

Come with me on this journey and I am sure you will find it extremely valuable in your eclectic cupboard of intervention tools. Get a large piece of paper or wallpaper. When you are ready, draw a brick wall, like the one below.

I would recommend about 24 bricks, and once drawn, think about what you would hope a child between the ages of 0 and 5 would experience consistently, predictably and repetitively.

Think Abraham Maslow's hierarchy of needs (1987), and in particular, the essential base of the pyramid – warmth, love, shelter, food and safety. Write each of these in any of the bricks you have drawn. Then, consider other experiences. These may include touch, hugs, play, education and stimulation. Continue to fill in the bricks with things like routine, boundaries, praise, happies, sads, role models and commentary, directions, toys and friends.

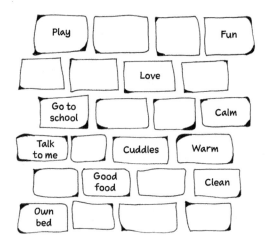

Once you have completed the wall, replicate it by using Jenga® blocks and, with a pencil, write each of the individual experiences on a brick (block). You should then build the brick wall so that there is a physical example for the next stage, which replicates the one that you drew.

Consider a child or young person who has experienced challenges such as trauma, loss and separation in their early life (aged 0–5). What experiences may not have occurred, or were not consistent, predictable or repetitive among the bricks you completed? You might have a child who was exposed to domestic violence in the family home, or neglect, lack of food, physical or emotional harm, or sexual harm, or a combination of all – for each that is lacking or not healthy, cross each brick out on the picture of a wall you drew on the paper. Typically, children I work for would have 'safe', 'boundaries', 'touch', 'warmth' and 'routine' crossed out, and 'food', 'toys' and 'love' half crossed out.

As one child told me, 'Of course we had food, or I wouldn't be here. It was the wrong food and I didn't always have food so this brick would be a crumbly one, that is not too strong.'

Once completed on paper, turn to your Jenga® brick wall and remove or half-remove the bricks (blocks) to correlate with the bricks crossed out or crumbly on the paper. The wall will start to collapse, and this becomes a great visual for the child to see the impact of their hurt and missed experiences. Once done, explain that the wall for a child of 0–5 is the foundation of life. I used to take children I worked with to building sites to look at the foundations that houses are built on. I would explain to them that the foundations are deep and strong to hold the weight of the house for a hundred or more years. The foundation of the child's first five years is the same, and we need to try and rebuild what might be broken, missing or crumbly.

The role of carers, whether foster, adoption, connected, guardians or birth, is to repoint the child's wall, to sometimes replace the bricks that are missing by providing the care and love and instruction that was absent. This rebuilding is possible if the owner of the wall and the repairer can attune together, and through relationship, therapeutically develop a new and strong foundation.

I was working with a 13-year-old boy in his seventh placement and his carer was a single female carer. The placement was not healthy, and both the boy and the carer were often competing with each other as to who was in charge. The boy found it very hard to self-care, to manage his behaviour, and reacted to the anger directed at him by the carer. For the carer's part, she would often shout and on occasion swear at him if he didn't do what he was told. Much of these arguments were around his hygiene and sleep. I introduced the wall exercise and after building the ideal wall, we began to talk about the boy's early childhood experiences. As we talked about his early life and how he had witnessed domestic violence, neglect and hunger, I heard the carer becoming upset. She then had a cry and as she did, the young person hugged her, and once she was settled in herself, we carried on the task.

I asked the carer what her task was, with reference to the broken wall, and before she was able to respond, the young person suggested that she needed to help him rebuild it. She turned to her foster child, apologized to him, and explained that she would try not to shout, and to explain and show what would be good care and help him to rebuild his wall.

I have also used the wall when working with adolescent girls who may have a 'need' to have a baby. In doing the wall about babies and young children's needs, there is a connection to their own early life experiences. I remember a child saying to me that a baby of seven months needs help to feed, comfort to sleep, skin cream on his bottom and to be clean and warm. This child then wrote on her wallpaper, 'My mum didn't know how to do this properly, so I need to make sure I know how and I am able to keep my child safe – maybe when I am 30!'

24

Scaffolding and the Trauma Bond

I use the wall activity to also help children to understand why their parents may have the challenges that they do, and that it is not about love. The children I work with often state that they are unworthy, that they feel unloved and that they are useless. These conclusions come from the reality of, for example, a parent continuing to take drugs – 'If they stopped, they could look after me' – or a parent remaining with a violent partner – 'If they loved me, why would they stay with someone that hurts them?'

To make sense of this, it helps to understand the notion of a trauma bond. Many believe that a trauma bond is a bond created between those who have suffered the same trauma – and in some ways, this is a fair assumption. However, a trauma bond is so much more than the experience of trauma; it is often survival. Although there appear to be many people who talk of the concept of a trauma bond, I would like to base my thinking on the work of Beverly James (2008). She was a very active contributor to trauma-informed practice before it became the mainstay it is now. I have slightly added to her explanation of the trauma bond so that I can use it in direct work with children and families.

Healthy-attached relationship versus trauma-attached relationship

As a quick note, I don't use the context of a slave relationship, but refer to it as a trauma-based relationship. In a healthy attached relationship, the person who has love for another attunes to their needs and contributes to their joy. To see them in this state provides pleasure and assurance – much like the love for your child, your partner or your parents. It is neither forced nor demanded; it is an emotional attunement for love.

Attachment (love)	Trauma bond
Attunement for pleasure and security	Attunement for survival
Focus on own wellbeing	Focus on other's needs
Obedience with some protest	Unwavering obedience
Checking in	Stay close or stay absent
Full range of emotions	Exaggerated expression of feelings
Cohesive and competent	Fragmented and incompetent

In an unhealthy trauma relationship, a person who needs to survive the threat from their partner, parent or family will attune to that person's requirements before being asked. Failure to do this may lead to the threat being acted on and pain as a result. To be safe is the only driving factor of this relationship, and as such, the attunement to the other is essential. It is forced and demanded, and if the person under threat sees it as effective, it becomes love and the only way forward. If we think about the concept of domestic violence – whether emotional, financial or/and violent – the way that the threat shapes the threatened person is to gain their trust, to make them feel they are the only one, to eliminate their support network and encourage dependence on them. Once the threat has succeeded in removing external connections, the threat can then dominate. The threat becomes the focus of need, a demand that must be met. The relationship is then shaped on meeting the need of the threat. Slowly, but surely, the threat becomes love, a sense of security and one that is supreme.

In a healthy-attached relationship of loving attachment, the loving person will focus on their need to be loved and provide for, to have attention and support. This focus on the loving person provides surety and safety, and if not feeling this, then the relationship can be questioned: Do you love me? Do you want me? Am I okay in this relationship? And if not, the loving person can leave and is freely able to do so.

In a trauma-based relationship, the loving person needs to focus on the threat, to meet their every need even if this does not meet the need of the loving person. Often this focus needs to be 100% and this might mean that the needs of the children in the relationship are also not seen or compromised. If the loving person has to focus on their threat, then reason, fairness, care and awareness dissolve in the need for the loving person to be safe. The focus becomes ultimate and all else becomes invisible. We often see this in family violence, where an aggressive parent violates their family and the non-aggressive parent cannot protect their children and often cannot see them.

When we talk about 'non-offending' parents, those parents who don't see abuse, the ill treatment of their children or themselves, we might feel incredulous that they didn't see this happening. It is perfectly feasible that a parent does not see the abuse of their child, or of themselves, if they are shaped to believe that they are loved, and that the hurt is not hurt but 'the care I deserve', and that the attachment has been shaped through the need to survive – 'I deserve to be treated this way; they have a right to do what they want and I have no right to challenge'.

In a loving attachment, when the loving person is asked to do something, it might be that the answer is 'no', or 'later'. This is a common reaction when we know that 'no' does not mean that the loving person will be hurt, or at risk; rather that we can say 'no'.

In a trauma-based relationship, when the threat demands, to say 'no' may prove too risky. To say 'no' is a danger, and so the loving person to the risk would respond in meeting the demand at whatever cost, and the demands over time seem, to the loving person, acceptable – 'I want sex', then the response is 'yes'; 'I want you to hit the child', the response is 'where?' To say 'no' would be impossible and very dangerous.

In a loving relationship, the loving person and the loved person want to stay connected, to feel available, and for this there must be 'checking in', the odd text to say how we are, to feel attached and to feel missed and belonging. Many of us who are in a loving relationship will connect when we are absent from each other, and hope that our partner will stay in touch with us.

When in a trauma-based relationship, checking in is a must. To account for each moment, each person you see and everything you do is crucial to the safety of the loving partner. To report in, to make known keeps us safe and, if your wellbeing depends on this, after time your belief is that this is the only way forward and you do it automatically.

With children of carers who have a trauma-based relationship experience, they learn either to limpet to their carer or to avoid. If you are a foster carer caring for an adolescent and it feels like you are really only offering 'bed and breakfast', you are not. The adolescent has learned that the only way to stay safe is to avoid family, intimacy – 'if I don't give, you can't take'.

Similarly, if you are caring for a young child and they seem to follow you around, they follow you not because if they can't see you then they feel abandoned, but if they can't see you, they cannot see the threat. In a way we might say, 'keep your friends close and your enemies closer'. If the child's internal working model tells them that adults are dangerous, why would you be any different?

In a healthy-attached and loving relationship, the loving person can express their full range of emotions. When sad they can be sad, when angry, angry and when silly, of course they can feel silly. If angry, their loved one does not have to become hurtful or abusive; they may respond with apology, conciliation or acknowledgement. In other words, if you are angry, sad, happy or bored, it is okay.

In a trauma-based relationship, emotions may be dangerous; to emote a feeling, a response or an opinion different to the one desired is dangerous, and so the safe thing to do is to emote to the needs of the threat. Children in this relationship of trauma learn to do the same, to suppress their emotions to be safe, to ensure that they do not betray their feelings as a potential danger. Often when caring for children who have experienced this hurt, we forget that they have been shaped to be careful, to see threat before safety. For these children, emotional intelligence is everything, and what you might see as an 'emotionless' child is really a wary child. In effect, an attuned child, but attuned to violence and threat instead of love and belonging.

In an attachment based on love, the person in love will attune to the other person – be that a partner, child, friend or parent – and anticipate their needs and provide what they can. They do this vigilance of relationship because it feels internally warming to see a loved one happy, content and their needs met – we feel good.

In an attachment based on trauma, the person who is threatened will attune to the other who is a threat, and seek to meet the needs of the threat before the threat becomes real. They attune by rigorous and sometimes blinded vigilance, far beyond the meerkat mode (Adkin and Gray-Hammond 2023) of vigilance. This is not to feel good, but to be safe. For those of you reading this book who work with children in care, and adults who have experienced care, it is a good idea to consider my '80/20 rule' – that the child is attuned to 80% of what is happening around them so that they can ready, respond, run or retire, whereas people caring for children attune to 20% as their placement does not have the potential to end.

To the scaffold, then – go back to your original wall picture and repeat it with the healthy bricks completed. Then, think with the child what their birth parent's experience as a child was – this information can be gleaned from the child's social worker, if felt appropriate. In my interventions, I have often interviewed the birth mother of children and have permission to share their story. If you were to make the Jenga® set, replicate the healthy wall and then, on the paper version, cross out the things missing from the parent's early childhood. This might be lack of safety, no toys, lack of boundaries and little praise.

Take the Jenga® blocks away as you copy the paper wall and the wall may collapse or become very wobbly. At this point, I would then narrate that, unlike their birth mum, they have lots of people around them to help. Maybe their birth mum didn't have people to help, or she didn't understand why people were wanting to help her. If her wall continued to be wobbly and broken, she might not be able to manage her world.

I would then explain to the child that some very old buildings in towns and villages, like churches and older houses, often have broken walls and so they need to be supported. They have scaffolding made of wood and metal, which is strong and secure. In some cases, this scaffolding is bigger than the wall itself and you can't quite make sense of the wall itself – it is lost. Then I would go back to the Jenga® wall that replicates their birth mum, and explain that she may have needed scaffolding to hide her broken wall. That the scaffolding would not be made of steel and wood, but something else that might take her away from the sadness she felt. Children get it very quickly – they tell me that the scaffolding might be made of drugs or alcohol, and some might be unsafe relationships.

When thinking about the child's journey, I may go on to narrate that if you were a child at home with your mother taking drugs, or in a trauma relationship, that social workers and others may be concerned for your safety. They might try and support your family and help mum to stop taking drugs or to leave the violent relationship. If your mum is very strong, she might do this, but if her scaffolds are taken away, she has the sadness of her broken wall. Sadly, we are not good at providing services to work with parents, and if the reality of the wall is too fragile, and the temptation to bring back the scaffold too great, then drugs are again being taken, or the establishment of another distractive behaviour to hide the reality of her wall. It is not about love, but about survival – the young people I talk to often get this and realize that it is not that they were not loved; it was survival behaviour to protect.

With the broken wall that is the birth mother's, put a scaffold against it to emphasize the point, and then ask the child how we might help them rebuild their wall so they don't need any scaffolding.

25

Internal Working Model Balance

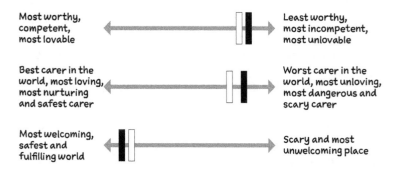

Most worthy, competent, most lovable ← → Least worthy, most incompetent, most unlovable

Best carer in the world, most loving, most nurturing and safest carer ← → Worst carer in the world, most unloving, most dangerous and scary carer

Most welcoming, safest and fulfilling world ← → Scary and most unwelcoming place

I find this intervention so helpful when working with children who are struggling with their internal working model (IWM). We have already discussed the concept of John Bowlby's notion of met and unmet needs (1988; see also Rose and Philpot 2004), but this helps me to illustrate the impact of the IWM for young people and their carers. The balance shown in the figure incorporates Bowlby's model of a healthy and an unhealthy blueprint of expectations. To the left is the healthy and to the right the unhealthy. If you copy this figure, don't include the markers. Consider your own balance of these three measures: How do you see your internal sense of self? How do those close to you relate to you and care for you? And lastly, how do you view the world and your place in it? Follow these guidelines.

The top line is a measure of your internal beliefs of you – do you feel lovable, able and worthy, or more unlovable, unable and worthless? Plot your measure on the scale. Most social care workers are more to the right than the left – I know I am. If you think you are the best since ever, go left to the left; if you think you are the worst of everyone, go right to the very right.

The middle line is a measure of your internal belief in those who have authority over you and your wellbeing. Plot your measure on the middle line. If you feel they are dependable, lovable, protecting and always acting in your best interests, go left; if you feel that they are uncaring, inconsistent, hurtful and unpredictable, mark to the right.

Finally, the bottom line – this is a measure of the world outside your 'front door'. Are you engaged, happy, secure and settled in the world? Do you believe you have a place and a space, and it is predictable? If so, go left, and if the feelings are opposite and the world does not feel safe and you don't feel you have a place, then go right.

Once completed, you should have a picture of your world view and you can then decide if this is okay for you, or if you want to change the balance. Like all these tools in this book it is the conversation and commentary you have while carrying out the task that will make the difference.

My worked example already mapped out the model for a case I was involved in – I will relate a narrative that is based on the case but not identifiable. On the figure, you will see six measures, two on each line. The filled black rectangle is the parent of the child and the non-filled rectangle is the 14-year-old daughter. The first measure is the internal world of the child and her carer. They completed their charts separately and were not aware of what the other said. Both have very poor views of self; the girl told me she was useless at everything, including school and friendships (especially her wish to be a boy). She felt invisible and insignificant. Her father scored lower than she, stating that she was the worst in her family, that she couldn't be as good as her siblings and was stuck in the area she lived in, which she found boring and insignificant.

The second measure was equally low. The girl explained that her father was never about, that she thought that he didn't want her and wasn't aware of her. The father had lost his connections with his family of origin and, since caring for his daughter, the friends he did have had all moved away – so he felt abandoned and mistrustful of having new friends.

The final measure is the world, and both scored towards the left, explaining that the world met their needs and they both felt wanted and important. Sadly, though, the girl did not get her needs met at home by her father or from extended family. However, older children did welcome her into their group; she shoplifted when told to, and did dangerous things to feel important, welcomed and needed. Her father also went straight to the left. He was a very successful man and was generous to his workforce, but he would not let them approve expenditure over a certain amount. This resulted in contact throughout the day and into the night, as he would troubleshoot and also protect his three companies.

If you can, when completed, look for opportunities for change when change is needed, and have those critical conversations. In this combination of case examples, the father needed to allow his employers greater responsibility and to hire a manager to act as protector of his companies so he could be home more and available to his child. His daughter needed to be supported in weaning herself away from the young people exploiting her, and once this happened, her father would be available to her and hopefully meet her need. If the balance on the bottom of the screen moved to the centre, then, in a short space of time, the middle balance would go towards the right in tandem, and the top line would eventually show the impact of love, care and availability.

This is not for everyone, but if you gave it a try, reflect on the thoughts and issues raised, and it should give you confidence in using the model. It might be helpful for you to consider what actions might be useful to move forward. This IWM chart can help to understand how children and young people can be vulnerable to exploitation such as sexual, criminal, county lines (drug trafficking) and/or violence. If you found that the child you completed the IWM with had not had their needs met internally, nor met by parent/family/carers, then who is available to meet those needs in the wider world? If a child's vulnerability is visual, spotted and targeted by those who might use them, then they are at risk.

Child sexual exploitation studies suggest that vulnerable children can interpret the act of exploitation as one of love – the attention, the receiving of gifts and money, alcohol and drugs to be thought of as special. Many children I have worked with have told me that at least they felt loved, important and wanted.

Of course, this is not new. Oliver Twist (Dickens 1838) is a fictional account of this IWM, and of exploitation. Oliver loses his home, is alone in the world and finds himself in London, with no food and no safety. He is spotted by the Artful Dodger and invited to go with him to see Fagan. The Artful Dodger is older than the other boys and not so useful, but has the patronage of Fagan as he brings boys to him. Fagan gives Oliver attention, importance, food, gin and lodgings, and in return he must go out and learn to 'pick a pocket'.

This IWM chart helps identify the risks and the factors in needs met and unmet. Then we can understand that some risks that we see our children take can be compared with the importance of the attention they crave.

26

Feelings Work

THE EMOTIONAL SELF

The following activities help to work on emotional literacy, emotional vocabulary and emotional expression.

Emotional themes

One way of working with feelings could be to identify with the child eight feelings that they have frequently felt; this might be angry, sad, happy, frustrated, bored, silly, lonely and confused. Think about these with your child and how these feelings make you all think, feel and do. If you can, share your own understanding of these feelings to act as an anchor for the child. You might want to consider times when these feelings were present and contextualize these with the emotions you share and how you recover from these.

Once done, consider a symbolic way of identifying these feelings. A good approach might be to think of a theme and relate the eight feelings to eight pictures. As an example, the theme could be cars, holidays, a funfair, the beach or weather. Here is an example using weather:

Happy		Angry	
Confused		Silly	

Love		Cross	
Anxious		Careful	

With these symbolic representations, be they animals, hairstyles, jumpers, shoes or plants, you can make copies and then have eight piles of picture feelings. As you talk about difficult things, the child can choose a picture to identify an emotion, or a series of emotions, from the piles of feelings. Most hurt children I have worked for hate being asked, 'How does that make you feel?', so a practical way of picking the picture rather than naming the feeling may prove helpful.

As you work you might find new or more specific feelings become identified, and so a new car or hairstyle will add to the legend created.

> I remember working with a 13-year-old girl who explained how angry she was at her friend for calling her a name. She selected a pepper picture to represent that she was angry at her (her themes were around food). Later we spoke of her father causing broken bones to her mother and she reached over for a pepper picture. I asked her if the feeling she had for her friend calling her a name was like her feelings towards the actions of her father to her mother, and she said she was furious at him.

We discussed that feelings and emotions are very different, and that a pepper for 'angry' might have lots of different kinds of pepper – less for cross and more for furious. She chose to use the commonly used one pepper, two pepper and three pepper identification – we learned that there are many shades to feelings and so built on emotional vocabulary.

Have a go at this activity. Do this with a child or a colleague. Write down eight feelings and then together identify a theme. Perhaps you agreed on hairstyles. Draw different hairstyles that relate to the feeling words and discuss why those styles have been experienced. Once complete, you could make feeling cards, or you could make lots of copies, or just use the name of the hairstyle as code for the feeling – 'I am feeling a little frizzy today – silly'; 'I felt bald – lonely' and so on.

In a book I edited and provided chapters for in 2017 (*Innovative Therapeutic Life Story Work*), I introduced another way of working on emotions and this has proved *almost* fool-proof. The first thing is to make emotional thinking fun and rewarding. My go-to is using Maltesers® (chocolate honeycomb-filled balls). In fact, my currency is chocolate when I work with children and young people who find conversations challenging. In Harry Potter's escape from Azkaban, he is being trained by Professor Lupin to use his Patronus – as he tries, he faces his fears – 'a Bogart taking the role of a Dementor' – and he is overwhelmed and starts to shake with fear. Professor Lupin gives him chocolate. The autonomic nervous system contains our fight and flight nerves (sympathetic) and these, when activated, get us ready to protect our 'self' (I always argue that each of us, at our most basic level, has a basic need to survive). The autonomic nervous system also contains another nervous system that causes a response to freeze, to become still and not be seen (parasympathetic). As the fight or flight is activated, the freeze is trying to calm, rest and digest – digest is the key word here, and chocolate is the ideal provision.

Sometimes children who have had difficult experiences can find any thinking about their past or emotions too dangerous. The following approach is based on ideas from children in this situation, and has developed through use over time. What we know is, it works!! You need Post-it® notes, a stopwatch (a phone timer works) and, for the adult, your internal child! This works well when you do this with a few more people – ideally a child and their carer.

Put the stopwatch timer on a minute countdown and then, on a big piece of paper or wallpaper, draw three large boxes – or two, if only two people are involved. Then ask those involved, including yourself, to write down in their designated box as many feeling words as you and they can in one minute – if there is a literary challenge, then one adult writes for the child. When this is done, we find that children will often list more than the carer, and this is really helpful. The average number of written feelings words tend to be around 12, although I have had a nine-year-old with 19 and an adult with 23 before.

If three of you are doing this work, the child, adult and worker, you might end up with 36 feelings in one minute. If you tried to do the same task by asking a child to talk about feelings, you may get 3 or 4, but if play includes a reward, such as stars, sweets or praise, then you will have so many more emotions to explore. Involving everyone makes healthy competition and emotional vocabulary discussion.

Once completed, share the words that have been written in the boxes and consider what are the same, similar or unique. Get everyone to write down each of their feelings in their boxes on a Post-it® note – so 'sad' on one, 'angry' on another, and so on. You should end up with 36 Post-it® notes with identified feelings written on each. Once done, fold each in half and half again, and place all of them in the middle of the table. Mix them up and then play the following three rounds.

Have everyone pick a Post-it® note each, and then read the note but don't tell anyone what word is on the note. Now, in turns, the first person explains the word they have without using the actual word written down. For example, if I said, 'I get this way when I don't get what I want', what would the word be? You might guess 'frustrated' – it is not, but I would now get a blank Post-it® note, write 'frustrated' on it, fold it twice and add this word to our pile of words on the table.

I would ask for you to guess again, and eventually you might say, 'angry' and I would say, 'yes'. Whoever guessed right would get a Malteser® and we then move to the next person to have a go. We only have up to three goes each. In this part of the activity, we are extending our emotional vocabulary, and having fun.

The next round, everyone picks a new Post-it® note, then reads the word, but does not tell anyone what it says. Then, turn-based, the word the person has must be used in a sentence that makes sense. If I have the word 'frustrated', I might say, 'I get frustrated when waiting for a bus and I am already late for work'. If everyone agrees that this is a good use of the word, then I get a chocolate. If not, I get to try again. This helps our emotional literacy...while still having fun! Play up to three rounds and then move to the final round.

The last round is the best round. Everyone picks a Post-it® note, but does not read it this time. When everyone has a note, each player places the unread note on their forehead – it should stick. Then, when everyone is ready, the first person has to guess the feeling written on their Post-it® note by guessing what everyone else is acting out. Those acting out must do so in silence and try and help the person guessing to get it right. The successful guess will mean that everyone gets a Malteser® and so it is a mutual reward.

This helps to identify emotional expression, but remember, pretending a feeling might look very different to expressing the real feeling.

> I found this when the child who helped me learn this process had the word 'angry' on his Post-it® note attached to his forehead. His carer and I were acting out silently what we thought were angry expressions. He guessed various words, but not the word 'angry'. His carer was not happy that he hadn't guessed the word, and, after a short while, she told him that he was not being fair and that he knew what the word was but was refusing to say it. He removed the Post-it note® and read the word 'angry' and, looking directly at his carer, said, 'But the actions you did are not like the way you look when you are angry at me.'

Just imagine the conversations and the attunement and potential that emotional discussions and congruence can give.

27

The Feelings Tree

NAME IT TO TAME IT

The feelings tree is an excellent way to support a child and their carer to emotionally attune, to name feelings and to make sense of them. It allows the opportunity for children to identify their own feelings, and it is useful for people who struggle to communicate their feelings. It is useful if a child is not travelling emotionally well and is unable to communicate this. The feelings tree is part of emotional intelligence and helps a child identify feelings on the inside and what they might look like on the outside.

Get an empty tissue box – you will need one for each person (say, child and carer). Then, decorate each box with some bright and fun stickers and colours so that it becomes a feelings box (having an individual box for each person promotes modelling from the primary carer and the child).

Using the same feelings words that you have come up with for '26. Feelings Work', put these words on a new set of Post-it® notes. If you like, you could purchase leaf-shaped Post-it® notes or cut out leaf shapes from the everyday square Post-it® notes.

Place the new leaf-shaped Post-it® notes in the feelings boxes so that each box has the same words in. Then, on an A3 piece of paper, draw a tree, and put the child's name at the bottom of the trunk. Get another A3 piece of paper and draw another tree, and put the carer's name in the trunk. You can have an A3 page for each person in the family, if it is helpful, but ensure each also has a feelings box with feelings leaves contained within. Once drawn, laminate all the A3 pages, or you can cover them with clear sticky-back plastic – the idea being that the paper is now strong enough to be used again and again, but also that it now has a shiny texture to allow the Post-it® notes to stick to it and to be removed.

As each person now has their own feelings tree, put the A3 tree pictures up in a place that is always available. I encourage people to place them in their kitchens – on a large fridge or cabinet door or on the wall.

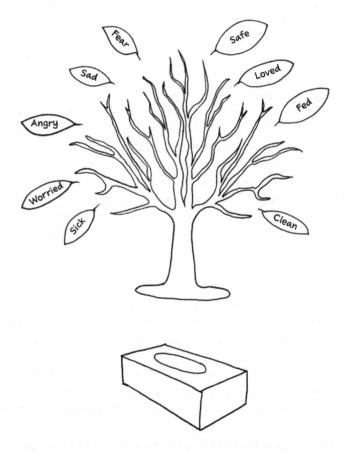

Over the next 10 working days (forget weekends, as they are always different), start with each morning. The carer goes first and chooses the leaf feelings that they are experiencing from their feelings box on their tree. They might be feeling tired, excited or happy. Once these are placed on the tree, the carer invites the child to do the same, to stick their leaf feelings on their tree. Once done, the carer takes a photograph of the trees for later in the day.

When the day is done, school over and around dinner time, the carer repeats the process of placing feelings that are held and taking away the feelings that are no longer felt – so the carer might feel content, thoughtful and calm, and so remove the tired, excited and happy leaves and replace them with the new feelings. The carer invites the child to do the same, and now they have a chance to see that changes in emotions are measurable. The carer takes a photograph for later.

In the evening, just before bedtime, the carer looks again at the trees to see if any new feelings are present and old ones to be removed. This time, once the child and the carer have sorted the trees, together they look at the previous tree pictures from the day and consider how things have changed for each of them over the day.

This activity has been so helpful with families where they have difficulty in understanding emotions and have challenges in the emotional communication between those in the household. After just these 10 days, the attunement of emotions and the discussion about these allows for a common language and ease of identification.

Carers will recognize an emotion before it becomes a behaviour, and children will identify a growing emotion. Name this and seek support to manage it. Dan Siegel introduced the phrase 'name it to tame it.'[1]

> As one child told me, 'I used to get really fuddley, and so I would attack mum and dad, but now we know that fuddley is the same as feeling anxious, mum and dad know this now, and we all get fuddley sometimes, but now we know what it looks like.'

John Gottman (1998) reminds me of the importance of families spending time talking about emotions, which helps their children to manage relationships, bullying and loss, and to make and maintain friendships.

This activity is a brilliant way to have emotion-rich dialogue.

---

1   www.youtube.com/watch?v=ZcDLzppD4Jc

28

Race Tracks

My job is not to force children to talk, but instead to give them the opportunity to do so. In this activity, I introduce two different ways of doing race tracks. The first is a great way to encourage discussions and memory work, and I have decided to illustrate the steps you need to follow:

- Step 1: Draw a race track, running track, etc., on a big piece of paper or on wallpaper.
- Step 2: Draw the start and finish line.
- Step 3: Give each participant a different colour.
- Step 4: The first person puts their pen at the start line, closes their eyes and begins to go around the race track with their eyes shut, but tries to stay within the lines.
- Step 5: When you go out of the lines, the young person or adult will tell you – draw a cross where you went outside the line.
- Step 6: Once everyone has had their turn, the person who won (or who went further without going outside the lines with their eyes shut) tells something about their story or about them in the present, or recalls one of their memories.
- Step 7: What is said about their story is written inside the race track.
- Step 8: To then restart the race, use the point where the furthest player went over the line, and everyone has their go from that point.
- Step 9: At the end of the game, when someone has crossed the finish line, there will hopefully be enough memories, stories and observations that the child or young person can be given a memory book.

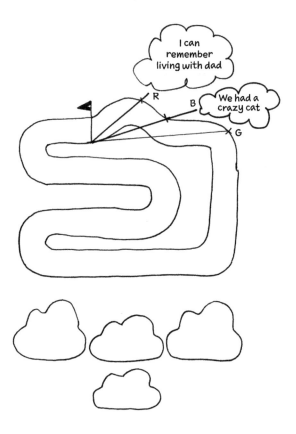

This easy-to-do, yet information-rich exercise has had many successful outcomes, from a 15-year-old completing every Formula 1 race track and having his own memory book, to a 5-year-old with a race track that was the length of a piece of wallpaper and took three sessions to complete.

The second way is to draw a race track and once done, to add the start/finish line. From here you ask, 'Who has won the race?' Most of the children I work alongside choose themselves as the race winner – they often draw themself as a car, a horse, a person or even a tortoise. Once done, I would then ask the child who they would like to have had in the race, and we add competitors and talk about them as we go through the co-created race scene.

Next, we talk about what the child won – a cup, trophy, money, glory and/or pride. Following this, I would ask if the race was fair, and if there were judges (the people we feel are honest and kind), who would they be? Finally, to see this brilliant win, I would ask the child who they would want to celebrate their success with.

This activity really helps to see the child's world and those people who impact on them, but also those they trust or believe.

For one child, we did the race track, and she chose horses. After adding other horses in the race, spectators and other incidentals, she drew a stable block and horse's 'poo' in the stables. The people who had to clean the stables out only had a spoon, and these people were those who had hurt and abused her. In other words, they only had a spoon to clear up a lot of horse manure rather than a shovel – and they deserved this awful task.

29

The Ishikawa Model (or the Herring Bone)

Dr Kaoru Ishikawa was a Japanese motor consultant for Toyota. He was asked to consider how to identify challenges for Toyota that could be overcome, and so make the cars more efficiently and cost-effectively. He came up with the Ishikawa model, which is more commonly known as the 'Herring Bone'.

I use the Ishikawa model more to problem identify and not to problem solve (although that does sometimes become a positive outcome). It is mainly for use with older children who are struggling in their world as it is versus where they would like it to be – for example, for the child who wants to go home because they are missing their brother or sister.

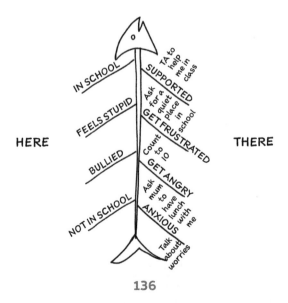

The idea is to think of somewhere the child is stuck.

Here: Where you are currently – in care.

There: Where you want to be – living back with mum.

Blockers (fish bones): what gets in the way of this happening?

As you identify the blockers with the child, write these at the top of the diagonal lines (the fish bones). As an example, things that block a child returning to their mother's care might be the Care Order, finance, resources, the child's behaviour, the mother's behaviour, and more. Hopefully you are following this and have now added the titles to the blockers between the 'Here' and 'There' points. With the model complete, think with the child, what could they do for each of the blocks that might reduce the problem, and place these ideas on the left side of each blocker by adding a line coming from the block at right angles.

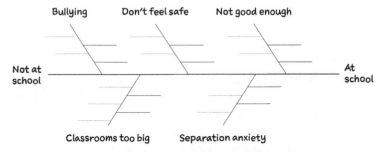

Fill in the lines on the left with what can be done by the individual; the lines on the right identify what others can do

These ideas and actions can be discussed as they materialize and thoughts and conclusions written on the far-left of the model. On the right side of the blockers write from the child's perspective what they think others could do to reduce the blocker, such as their social worker, family and you, the therapist. Once done, the ideas and actions can be discussed as they materialize, and thoughts and conclusions written on the far-right of the model.

Have a go at completing this model, and as you do, reflect on the problem identification that is happening. You could choose to think of a child not in school and getting them to school; a child self-harming and no longer self-harming; sexual harmful behaviour and no longer sexually harming. If this is too confusing, think of something less challenging, such as having an old car and wanting to buy a new one! This method helps the child or young person to understand the complexity of the situation. As the Ishikawa model builds, it is usual to identify plans, targets and objectives as they emerge. The way that I use the Ishikawa model focuses on identifying complexities and challenges, rather than as a problem solver, although that is also possible. Often the child who completes the task can see the complexities of the situations, but also, more importantly, they can make sense of why, and if the why can be identified, this can be the most powerful outcome of recovery.

A working example of this approach could be seen when working with a young person who did not want to be in his residential home; he wanted to be in a foster home. He had heard that fostered children can stay in care until they are 21, but in residential care, you had to leave by your 19th birthday. He understood that he had challenging behaviours and other needs that might be a difficulty for carers to meet, but was angry that his social worker was not arranging for him to be moved. His requests had been dismissed and, as such, he began to blame the residential staff and his social worker, and convinced himself that he and they were just not good enough.

His blockers included his medical needs, his behaviour and his mental health, alongside the scarcity of finding carers with medical knowledge, with previous concerns of his criminal behaviour and his drug use. Together, we addressed each blocker, with the left side 'What can he do?' and the right side 'What can others do?' After a while he was able to see the complexity of the situation and the reality of why this wasn't possible for him.

In a similar case, I had a child interrupt the process and state, 'It's not going to happen, is it?' and I asked if he could see why. The Ishikawa model helped this young person to see the problems, to identify the challenges and whether a cause or response could be found to resolve it. It is possible to consider that the realization of a 'no' could cause challenging behaviour in itself, but I find the opposite. Young people can accept something when it is talked through and visual. Once this is experienced, we can then see what else might be possible. I am pleased to say that the outcome of both these cases was that they found community resources that were available for them but not thought about until we completed the Ishikawa model.

It is really fantastic when someone carries out an Ishikawa model and then responds, like a young person I was working with. She suddenly said, 'Hey Richard, what you mean is that there are things I can do and there are things I can't. I am going to concentrate on the things I can do and hope others will do their part' – a little like 'Grant me the serenity to accept the things I cannot change, the courage to change the things I can, and the wisdom to know the difference'.

Don't discount what you can do – when I have a difficult case, I use the Ishikawa model, and you could too. I might get a referral that asks me to address attachment, trauma or therapeutic life story work, and so I acknowledge where the child is. I then ask where the commissioner of my work wants me to get to (the 'Here' and 'There'). I will try and work out what is getting in the way by addressing the challenges. Then I will identify what I can do and what I may need others to do – my actions on the left and the actions for others on the right.

With this visual, I can then go to the other resources and providers and ask if they could do what I need, and if not, I can go back to the commissioner and state, 'I can't do what you have asked as I, or other provider services, cannot meet the need.' I may possibly offer a different aim and objective that is possible, and it is more likely that I can then engage in the best interests of the child.

30

Trauma-Based Behaviour Table

We can use many problem-solving communication tools. The one I like to use is a trauma-based behaviour table, which you can see here.

Trauma background	Trauma-based behaviour	Behaviour outcomes	Reaction to behaviour	Response outcomes	Reflection on think, feel, do	Response for next trauma-based behaviour

The first column identifies the trauma background of the child – this could be sexual, physical, neglect, emotional harm, domestic violence, cultural trauma, and so on. The second column identifies the expected trauma-based behaviours we expect to see from those who carry the traumas identified. An example might be sexual harmful behaviours, defiance, overly compliant, aggressive to female carers, etc. Importantly, at this point do not enter the presented, just the expected. The third column identifies the presented behaviours that are on show; these might be the expected or they might be unique – such as targeting siblings, attacking carers or harming others; it might be self-harm, sexual exploitation, and so on. These first three columns are there to identify the child's presentation. If you have done '18. The Behaviour Tree' you could look at the roots for the trauma-based background and the leaves for the actual behaviour.

The fourth column is to identify the reaction of the adult who experiences the behaviour – importantly this has to be the reaction and not the response. Was there disgust, exasperation, fear, aggression? This fourth column helps to identify how the behaviour is received, and as with the monster behaviour being used to protect, does it work? The fifth column is to identify the response to the behaviour presented – the consequence, boundary, escape or counter-transference. Once these columns have been completed, we can then reflect on the behaviour and response, and whether what occurs is actually helpful, unhelpful or learned responses that have no capacity for change.

The sixth column concentrates on the ideal of 'think, feel, do' and should reflect the child's presentation, the carer's response and together develop alternative strategies to create mutual understanding and change. This then leads to the seventh column and the agreement of what will happen the next time the trauma-based behaviour is presented. This hopefully agreed response will allow new thinking that is achievable, visual, relatable and, most importantly, simple.

It is essential that the new thinking is given a chance to work. Too often advice is given and then thrown away as it doesn't work the first time. In my experience, this is like the lid of the glass we spoke of in attachment theory (see '1. Serve and Return') – it will work, it won't, it will, it will, it won't, and then hopefully it will!

31

Triangles

Often children need the chance to tell their story and how they see things that happen around them. It is also helpful to see how the child sees the view of the adult involved.

Problem:	What is the issue?
Child's needs/view:	What has happened?
	What do you need to be successful? Or safe?
	How do you think the teacher saw this?
Capacity/view:	What do you think your teacher is able to do to keep everyone safe?
Intervention required:	What needs to be done? What can I do?

Once the table is completed by the child, the following table is then completed by the carer/teacher:

Problem:	What is the issue?
Carer/teacher's needs/view:	What has happened?
	What do you need to be successful? Or safe?
	How do you think the child saw this?
Capacity/view:	What do you think your child is able to do to keep safe?
Intervention required:	What needs to be done? What can I do?

With both views now visual, it is possible to consider how each regards the same problem, what they see that is similar and different, what each person thinks would help them together and separately. Rather than confrontational, irrational or confusing, this model supports potential change. Doing this activity with multiple people included within a situation gives you, the intervener, a perspective of all those different people's understandings of a challenging situation.

Draw a triangle on a blank sheet of paper. If, for example, a student and their teacher have a challenge around a behaviour outburst in the classroom (this is something I am very familiar with – the triangle provides two different perspectives to see what is in common and whether there is some clarity or not), write in the middle of the triangle the behavioural challenge (in one of my examples the child had thrown a book across the classroom and the book had hit the teacher and another child).

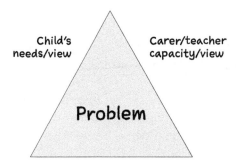

I would then meet with the child, and with the triangle template would ask how the child saw the problem. I would reflect with the child on how they saw the lead-up and the event as well as the aftermath. The statement leading to the discussion would be, 'My job isn't to tell you off, you have loads of people who do that. My job is to help you and others to make sense of what happened and how we can make it right.'

Once the views are heard and written on the left side of the triangle, I would then ask how the child might consider their teacher's reaction and the role of the teacher in the classroom. I do this by asking the child to pretend that they are in the teacher's shoes, and whether they can see, feel and think as if they were the teacher.

This mentalization exercise is really helpful as the child can imagine the space and, in many cases, will have eureka moments as they appreciate the challenges that are present. I have had children say, 'He cannot make himself heard', 'He needs to keep everyone safe', 'He has to help everyone learn', 'It is hard to make sure that everyone is okay in the classroom' and 'I would be angry if I had had a book thrown at me'.

We would write the comments down on the right-hand side of the triangle and together compare the left and right views. Finally, I would look at the bottom of the triangle, where the intervention is considered. With the child's contribution I would reiterate that my job is to help support this situation and to help them and to help the teacher. 'What can I do to help?'

Hopefully, the child will come up with some great ideas. These often include 'We could explain that I was angry at John because he was saying my mother didn't want me and that is why I am in care' to 'If the teacher could be told that I don't mean to get so angry, I just can't keep up with the class and it is too noisy for me'. With the completed child's version, I would go to the school and repeat the same process with the teacher – seeking their views on the right side of the triangle, and then the mentalization of the child from the teacher on the left side.

Finally, I would help the teacher to consider the 'intervention required' and ask how I might be helpful. All of the conversation would be written on the paper as it was materializing, using the triangle as the model.

With both completed triangles, place the two triangles together side by side and work out what they have in common. Look and see where there are other reflections and ideas and what intervention might be required. Then arrange a meeting with the child and the teacher, for everyone to have the opportunity to reflect, to present and to make sense of what happened and what could be done differently the next time.

I use this approach often, and once everyone feels calm and heard, great congruent plans can come forward to manage the classroom challenges and improve the relationship between the adult and child. This model also works with carers, social workers, parents and others as a reflective activity.

32

Brain and the Second-Year Attachment Cycle

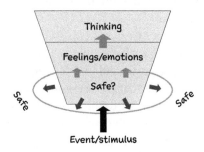

I have based this intervention on work from Dr Bruce Perry (Perry and Winfrey 2021) and Paul MacLean (1990) (although MacLean's triune brain theory is no longer taught). Although Dr Perry introduces the Neurosequential Model of Therapeutics (NMT) construct as a multilayered brain going bottom up, I have found it useful to reduce the levels to the original three sections, as in the figure here:

SAFE = The lowest part of the brain is the old brain, sometimes referred to as the reptilian brain, and it is responsible for our fight or flight response, our breathing, etc.

FEELINGS/EMOTIONS = The mid-brain comprises our limbic system, where our feelings emanate and resolve.

THINKING = Our cortex, or highest part of the brain, is where our experiences support our unique construct of the 'making sense and the why' brain.

I have deliberately simplified the descriptors so they are easily understood by all. The brain isn't, of course, so perfectly organized as this, but it helps to think about the function and organization of certain parts.

Consider that babies through to toddlers and into early adolescence will operate 'bottom up' – 'Am I safe?' 'What do I feel?' and 'What do I think?' – and adults, in the main, operate 'top down' – 'What do I think?' 'How do I feel?' 'Is it safe?' For example, think about the two-year-old in the supermarket. If the child sees something they want, they may try to go ahead and take it or insist that their carer provide it for them. The carer responds by saying 'No!' Now a 'no' for a two-year-old is a challenge; the child may need to test that boundary and, as a result, will respond to the 'no' as if it were a threat – 'You are not supposed to say no!'

If you currently have a two-year-old, or remember when you had care of a child this age, you will no doubt be familiar with this 'protest'. I can certainly remember my children testing me, and admittedly, in some cases I failed drastically – becoming forever the softy to my partner's clarity! This response to the 'no' can be seen when the child tries to grab, demand, shout, hit, and with some children end with (or even begin with) a full-on tantrum – as my mum used to say, to do the dance of the dying fly!

In reality, the child has lost their internal control and is no longer able to keep their 'self' safe. I am going to summarize, in very simple terms, Dr Perry's concept of safe, safe, safe – that when a child is overwhelmed, their survival brain detaches from their feeling and thinking brain/system and their survival behaviour now activated seeks only to protect the self. In the brain 'rhombus' figure you can see the arrows exploding outwards from the safe brain.

Dr Bessel van der Kolk (1998) suggested that trauma occurs when a person's internal and external world are overwhelmed and fear is translated into trauma. A child having this moment of feeling unsafe will develop a response that works for them, especially if they are not coping and it seems that the carer isn't either. Their internal world has failed to protect them, and their external carer, their external world, has not been strong enough. If and when this happens, the child has what they have shaped and worked for them in the past – the coping strategies and defence mechanisms that are effective and structure their safety valve.

Let's get back to if you have the two-year-old responding to the 'no' – they lose their internal control, so what do you do? Hopefully, as a caring adult, you will see the distress that the child feels and you would understand that the child no longer feels safe or can self-regulate and so calm. The child needs their caring adult (you) to pick them up, hold them to your chest, and calmly commentate that they are safe, that all is good, so co-regulating the young child. Once beginning to settle, as your commentary slowly calms the child, the child responds to your safe by understanding that when they can't feel safe the adult will protect them and they don't need to feel alone.

As carers, we all have this duty of care, to demonstrate and re-demonstrate protection, attention, guidance and safety. Once this is experienced and repetitive similar responses are reliable, the child has confidence in the boundary set by the parental figure as a notion of consistent, predictable and repetitive safe – 'When I don't feel safe, my carer will keep me safe'. The diagram here has a circle containing the red arrows and the word 'safe' written alongside. The circle is symbolic of containment, explaining visually that 'I can contain you when you cannot', which translates to a soothing therapeutic message of reassurance.

When I work with carers around the challenging behaviour of their children, I remind them of this concept of the brain – why is the child behaving like they are? Is it because they are unsafe and they perceive that the carer cannot keep them safe? As mentioned a few times in this book, as one child said, 'If I am in school or at home and I don't feel safe, I try people out to see if I am safe; if they can keep me safe, I am safe. If they can't, I am not safe; I become an angry animal, an angry lion, an angry me.'

Many of the children I work with are not so assured, secure and safe. If the adults around them are not sure how to manage this, or react with anger, punishment or dismissal, this demonstrates to the child that when they cannot cope, the carer also cannot cope. If this is experienced over a period of months, the child realizes that when they can't keep safe, their carer cannot protect and defend them. We, parent, carer or practitioner, need to create a ring of safety around the child, a shield of confidence. So when we pick up the reactive child and say, 'It's okay, I'm here, It's safe, we are safe' until the child calms down and this action is a familiar response that the child can see, experience and feel safe from, then the child will start to understand that the people around them are able to keep them safe; they can help them co-regulate, to help to activate their feeling and thinking brain.

If the child we are working for did not get this protective care in their early years, but were sadly left bereft, they do not look to the protection that the carer can provide, but learn that fear is a danger and something that they have to manage alone. Those arrows you see in the brain rhombus coming out of the safe brain become bigger, more effective and, in some of my children and young people I work with, it becomes a fixed, go-to 'protect mode'. The child has no expectation of support or the effectiveness of the adult to hold safe.

In attachment theory, not many people in the social care world are aware of the second-year attachment model (Levy and Orlans 2014), although the first-year attachment model is more familiar to all. Here I have taken Levy and Orlans' two models (2014). The first year is about survival and need; the second is about wants and safety! It is this second year that interests me the most – how we relate to our wants and how these are managed. In this second-year model, 'wants' replaces 'needs', 'distress' with 'boundary' (carer's), testing of the boundary (child testing), and feeling safe then connects with safety.

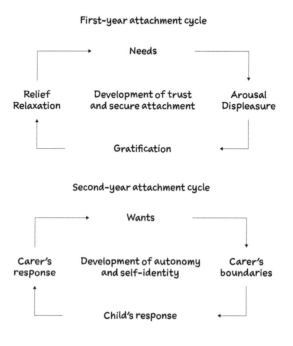

First-year attachment cycle

Needs

Relief
Relaxation

Development of trust
and secure attachment

Arousal
Displeasure

Gratification

Second-year attachment cycle

Wants

Carer's
response

Development of autonomy
and self-identity

Carer's
boundaries

Child's response

In this second year, many traumatized children have learned that the adults around them cannot keep them safe, will not, or cannot, install a boundary and, as a consequence, are not able to provide external protection when the child feels internally attacked.

'If a carer cannot keep me safe, then I will have to develop my own safety' – invariably this will be big, powerful and effective action in the moment, but not helpful for the longer term, where little is learned. Eventually, by the time the child enters education, they have their own effective 'protect mode' – the circle of safety from the carers has been replaced by the 'protect mode' that works.

We might have the situation of the seven-year-old who hits out and causes chaos when feeling threatened. The child needs to understand that we are there to help them feel safe – not shamed for the behaviour they have learned, but accepted for who they are. It is then our task to support the child and to work together on finding more effective ways to replace the 'protect mode' to be helpful for all, or, in the best outcomes, to help the child understand they don't need the protect mode as adults will keep them safe, if allowed to.

Winnicott (1960) says it is the job of the therapist to hold the pain of the child. I believe that our role is to show the child that they cannot overwhelm us, that we can be strong and clear and honest. If a child or young person becomes angry or escalated in session, we need to be a strong adult, to hold the boundary and to say through words and actions, 'It's okay: my job is to keep you safe'.

When the child calms, it provides the opportunity to help everyone reflect on the event that has taken place, to not only reflect on our feelings, but also our thinking and doing. As we all are aware, when anyone is in a state of survival, we are too busy to be able to listen, reflect and change. The art of reflection can be the most effective and meaningful next step to make sense from all perspectives and think on what we might do differently next time.

Using the brain image from the beginning of this activity, I find that older children really benefit from the most challenging of events, as you take them through the process and there is no room for shame or blame. If you recall from earlier in this book, Dr van der Kolk (1998) proposes that trauma occurs when the internal world is overwhelmed and the external world cannot cope. This use of the brain model will help normalize the existence of the learned behaviour, and also encourage new thinking that there are external worlds that can keep them safe.

33

Play as a Coolant

FIGHT, FLIGHT OR FREEZE

Often when working with children and young people about challenging events in their stories or in their current life, the act of reflecting can be overwhelming as their protection of self is activated with the reality that surfaces. Helping children to talk about their emergency response systems can be achieved through the earlier exercise of monsters and ghosts (see '17. Monsters and Ghosts'), but older children might prefer to talk in more biological terms.

Each of us has a resource within us that is coiled (more often with traumatized children), ready for action. This reaction, or safety valve, is not a conscious process but survival, and we know, thanks to films such as *Inside Out*, that the concept of fight, flight or freeze has become more widely known. I try not to make things too scientific, as the use of the complicated words for complicated actions becomes outside the reach of those involved. Here is a more simplistic way to explain it – while we are talking films, Forrest Gump and his 'Simple is as simple does!' is always my intention. When I failed my English Language exams at school, my teacher told me that the big problem was that my writing style was more like a 'tabloid than a broadsheet'... after four books and countless papers, I am so glad I didn't change my writing style. It may infuriate some of you, especially with my poor grammar (I apologize), but I hope it makes the content more understandable and, more importantly, 'reachable'.

Fight or flight was a term introduced by the US physiologist Walter Bradford Cannon (1871–1945), and popularized in his book *Bodily Changes in Pain, Hunger, Fear and Rage* (1929). This unconscious response is embedded in our brain and represents a genetic wisdom designed to protect us from harm. This response starts in an area of the brain called the hypothalamus, which, when stimulated, initiates a sequence of nerve cells that then communicate a chemical release that provides the energy and force needed for our body to fight or run. Cannon proposed that all humans are able to recognize an imminent threat to their survival and will unconsciously respond by altering their physiological state.

The cell sequence begins in the amygdala, the part of the brain that, among other things, is a little like a radar identifying threat and fear. When there is a threat or danger, the amygdala responds by sending signals to the hypothalamus, another part of the brain that communicates with the nervous system, which is autonomic. 'Autonomic' is a clever word for 'does it itself' – it acts automatically, without anyone making it happen – it simply does what it does without your permission or awareness.

The autonomic nervous system is actually part of a bigger collection of nerves that go on to connect with the peripheral nervous system and, in turn, the central nervous system. The central nervous system feeds information between the brain and spinal cord, and the peripheral nervous system goes from the brain and spine to everywhere else.

Have I lost you yet?

I am sure I haven't – it just means that part of your wiring goes to different parts of you; some need thinking and doing, and others just do! The area we are interested in is the area that can make it hard for others to understand behaviour. Let's concentrate on the autonomic nervous system, which I will refer to from now on as the ANS. This system has two components: the first is the excited one, the sympathetic nervous system and the other, the cool and relaxed one.

When you feel at risk, or you remember a time when this has happened and it feels like it is happening again, you may find that your body and your heart begin to tell you that you need to fight or run. This physical and emotional change is sudden and can be hard to manage, and before you know it, the trauma has its hold. When your ANS is stimulated, your body releases adrenaline and another chemical called cortisol into your blood to give your body a boost. Adrenaline and cortisol are produced by small glands on the top of your kidneys, and when the chemical is released as a need communicated by the hypothalamus, the effect is speedy. First of all, your heart starts to beat faster; you may have this happen when you are about to go on a roller coaster or somewhere scary like a ghost train!

As your heart beats faster, it pumps oxygen-rich blood to the places that need it the most – the brain and the major muscles that might help you fight or flee. You will then experience your chest expanding – your breathing gets faster as you are providing more oxygen to your blood; your eyesight gets very good as your brain is trying to identify the danger, and so the middle of your eye, the pupil, gets bigger, more light is let in and you can see really clearly. It is not only your eyes, though; your ears twitch as you strain to hear any signs that might protect you or give you a chance to escape.

With all this happening, your blood is also getting thicker as your brain assumes that you might be wounded, and so the thick blood will help clot any bleeding, and your skin goes all goose bumpy as the energy directs to essential places. Finally, the chemical endorphins will take some of the pain away as the hurt is not felt while the fight or flight is occurring. Usually, your body will return to normal after 20 to 30 minutes, if things are calm.

The ANS consists of a second system called the parasympathetic nervous system. This drives you to avoid fighting or running as this won't work, and so stimulates a shutdown designed to freeze everything. 'Freeze' is offered as a third unconscious response to a survival threat, suggesting that the human being would recognize the threat, calculate the risk of response, and work out that it was best to shut down the body to a minimum so as not to be seen or heard.

Think about a rabbit half-way across a road; it sees headlights and stops still. The rabbit senses its impending doom and will unconsciously stay unmoving. It will reduce its breathing, and hope that it cannot be seen as the headlights pass. In reducing its heartbeat, it enters a freeze process, just like you and I might do if we were in the dark – we can't see anything, but there is a noise in the corner of the room. In shutting down the system, you slow your heart rate and breathe very quietly, or even hold your breath for a period, which for some may cause fainting. Your chest does not rise and fall (the threat might hear this), and so you take very quick and silent breaths. Your eyes are closed and so the danger is not visualized, and sometimes you may cover your ears to stop hearing the threat.

I find this discussion so helpful for my children, as they start to understand that the hurting, the running and even the frozen watchfulness is understandable and present for everyone. I often go on to explain that when the flight and fear is happening, the body and the brain are so clever, that the parasympathetic nervous system is in battle with the sympathetic nervous system to calm it down, and that is where the carer becomes involved, with soft, safe commentary and the simple language of calm.

The parasympathetic nervous system is often referred to as the 'rest and digest' system, and that is why food is often needed after a fight or flight situation. Some of my children will actually grab food and munch away as we talk about difficult things. For those of us brought up on Harry Potter, in *Harry Potter and the Prisoner of Azkaban* (Rowling 1993), Harry is being taught how to use his Patronus, and when it goes wrong, Professor Lupin gives him chocolate for him to recover (supporting his parasympathetic nervous system to succeed in resting him).

I tend to talk with children about these 'F's of fight, flight or freeze. I haven't introduced other theories here, such as Stephen Porges' Polyvagal Theory (2001), or the notion of 'fawn' that Peter Walker discusses in his book *Complex PTSD* (2013) (my reasoning simply falls on the concept of the unconscious saving the day). Many children I work with fawn, either as a result of experiences of domestic violence, shame-based care experience, or, where it has been safer to disconnect from self and meet the needs of the threat and any other that might become a threat. If it works and if it works again, fawn becomes their go-to behaviour, and the need to people please becomes their sanctuary. Where do coolant games come in to our communicating with traumatized children? All the action, as it were, in the ANS is in the brainstem and the lower part of the brain, so when talking about the trauma, the brain is unbalanced towards the lower part.

Games are more typical frontal lobe activities, at the top and front of our heads, and with games, we can balance the impact we are having with the lower brain with quick-to-play games. Some of these have already been introduced in this book, such as '10. The Box Game', tic-tac-toe and card games.

Like an engine in a car, coolant stops the car overheating, and games and play provide the same for working with hurt children and young people. Speaking of coolant and cars, TBRI (Trust-Based Relational Intervention®) (Purvis and Quails 2020) has the 'engine plate' among many great ideas of calmer classrooms. I was introduced to this by a brilliant social worker in the Department of Human Services in Oregon in the USA.

The engine plate is a simple tool that helps us all to explore how we are travelling during the session/class or intervention we are engaged in. It is simple to make and simple to use but brilliant for regulation and co-regulation. I use a cardboard picnic plate and, with a pen, divide the plate into three sections – colour one section red, one green and one amber (like traffic lights). Then write 'OKAY' in big letters in the green section, 'NOT OKAY' in big letters in the red section, and finally 'WOBBLY' in big letters in the amber section.

With a split pin, push the pin's arms through the centre of the upside-down plate so that the arms of the split pin poke through to the coloured side of the plate. Then, push the arms down together to make an hour hand as if it was a clock – now you have an engine plate. As the child is in the session, they can, when needing to, indicate if they are running in the green and 'OKAY', tipping into the amber and feeling 'WOBBLY' or desperately in the red and struggling 'NOT OKAY'.

I used these plates in the enforced lockdown during the Covid-19 pandemic, when some of my work went online, and it was invaluable. This is a simple resource that can communicate quietly and purposefully how we are – and as a quick suggestion, we can all make use of an engine plate to regulate our busy world.

On the same theme as coolant games is the value of using music to calm when difficult subjects need to be discussed. In '1. Serve and Return', I talked about the attachment process using glasses. I would like to pick up the theme of the heartbeat and music as a theme for co-regulation and creating calmer therapeutic environments.

I find playing music during intervention sessions with young people can assist in keeping the sessions focused, on task, and free of potential overwhelming episodes. As in Eye Movement Desensitization and Reprocessing (EMDR), the movement of the eye following a finger, or rhythmic drumming or finger tapping, can occupy the senses. This allows the person to recall traumatic events and the impact left without the overwhelming anxiety and fear that might ordinarily accompany it. Shapiro (1989) developed a series of interventions to assist trauma recounting, and the technique relies on rhythm.

If, while in the womb, the forming baby is regulated by the rhythm of their mother's heartbeat, I often refer to this as the baby's unique rhythm of life. If, during challenging sessions, you play heartbeat-regulated music, such as rap music (without the words) or classical music, the child will hopefully regulate to the music as their heartbeat co-regulates to the beat of the music and not follow the stories being shared. Similarly, if you speak in a slow, melodic way, the child's heart will regulate to your voice and calm as you engage. Dr Dan Hughes is a master of this, using his voice and the rhythmic cadences to soothe the children he works with. I hope, in some small way, that I do the same (Hughes, Golding and Hudson 2019).

A metronome works particularly well for children or young people who have post-traumatic stress disorder (PTSD), or even a clock with a noise that is pleasant, but that counts each second as a dependable rhythmic beat. As already mentioned, American veterans are often advised to use a metronome, set at 72 beats per minute, so that when they have night terrors, their heartbeat will follow the metronome rather than the horror of the nightmare. Indeed, science has moved rapidly, and Apple Watches and iPhones now have NightWare, a process of sensing an increase in heartbeat as a nightmare begins; they use pauses rhythmically to stir the sleeper away from the nightmare without waking them.

In residential settings, we can capitalize on this phenomenon by playing music that is heartbeat-regulated at the end of the day. In schools, it can be helpful to play music rather than to isolate the child when they lose their internal control; with the constant, consistent and repetitive beat of the music, the opportunity for the heart to calm quickly is there, and studies have shown that this simple quiet and musical rhythmic beat can support calmer classrooms (Carlson *et al.* 1998).

If you go on the internet and search 'heartbeat-regulated music' you will find music-only versions of rap music that has beats of 60–65 per minute. Playing this beat quietly, and allowing the methodical, predictable and repetitive cadence of calm to be experienced, may be soothing for the child and for you.

Only a few months ago I was working with a child who needed to talk about the death of their birth mother. They knew that this would be difficult and, up to the session we were engaged in, had tried to talk to bereavement therapists and had not managed to complete those sessions. We talked about music and what he liked and what I liked, and we agreed that we would play music on volume 2 of a Bluetooth speaker. It was accepted that we could not change the music, the volume or turn it off, but that we would listen for a few moments and then we would talk about his mother.

This was an amazing session, as he spoke of his hurt, of finding his mother dead, and the worry that he was not able to help her. The music seemed to provide surety and comfort, and I thoroughly recommend using music this way as it has been specifically helpful if you are talking about death, or of a child or young person's abuse background.

34

Transference and Counter-Transference

Melanie Klein (1920) introduced the concept of transference and counter-transference when considering clinician and client inter-actions during psychoanalyst sessions. In a very brief synopsis, the client may transfer to the clinician their hurts, anger and frustrations – therefore transference. The clinician has to be mindful that this transference is the client's hurt, and not an attack on the clinician. However, transference may feel like an attack, and in defence, the clinician might react to the transference by responding defensively, or even to attack the client – this is called counter-transference.

Why introduce this in a book about communication? Well, all behaviour is communication, and transference is how a person may communicate their pain. There have been times when I have worked with children who seem to manage well at school, but when it comes to home, things can be very uncontained.

Take a moment to think about a child at school who has experi-enced trauma, feels they are not good enough and lives with internal shame. Then consider how amazing they are when they survive the school day, despite the pressures, the potential teasing, proving, com-paring and defending that is their everyday journey. Imagine that this child has learned that they must hold it all in, to not let things show, to avoid the attention and potential of failure (which may well be their belief of being not good enough).

By the time that child gets home they are exhausted and disor-ganized, they know that home is predictable, and hopefully their parental figures will be able to manage them. The exchange below shows the process of transference and counter-transference, and once it plays out, the environment is heightened for any others who might join in.

> Carer greets the child with a 'Hi, did you have a good day at school?'
>
> Child already disorganized responds, 'It was rubbish and I hate you for making me go.'
>
> Carer responds, 'I only asked how it went, there is no need to be rude!' Defending posture.
>
> Child retorts, 'It's all right for you! You just sit down watching TV and having fun. I hate you.' Insecure behaviours displayed.
>
> Carer feels need to react more firmly, 'How dare you say that! I clean your room, wash your clothes, I don't get a moment. If you weren't here, it would be so much easier.'
>
> Child becomes confused and angry and says, 'I wish I was somewhere else; at least I could be looked after properly and not in this dump!'
>
> Carer can only interpret that the child's behaviour is defiant, but also feels angry and upset, and now feels a little like the child had when they came into the home.
>
> Child feels blamed and shamed, but recognizes their carer is too angry, and so takes themself away from the situation.
>
> Carer and child both feel bad, and if someone else comes to the home, they may also be swallowed up by the transference and counter-transference.

Making someone feel bad just because you feel bad plays out in many families and schools, and the sad thing is that much of this can be avoided. When I work with these situations, I use whirlwinds to picture the transference – in this image the first whirlwind is the child and the second is the carer.

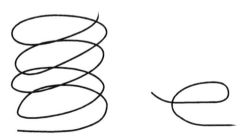

As the interplay escalates, the whirlwinds rise as each feeds the other. Eventually the whirlwinds are at their most powerful and the child and carer are no longer able to listen to each other.

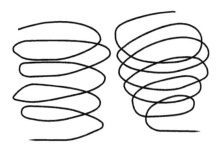

When I draw the whirlwinds, I add in the strands the details of the arguments, similar to the dialogue. Once mapped out, I would ask the carer to consider what might happen if they didn't journey on their whirlwind. If they stopped at the first whirlwind and said calmly, 'I am not coming up with you. I will stay calm and when you are ready, I'm here.' This is not easy to do, but as long as the carer can visualize not losing their internal control, and can concentrate on maintaining calm, the child will see this and not lead or follow the escalating loss of control. It is hard, but not impossible, and the role modelling will support the child in finding a calmer way to communicate.

In many cases where I have helped this to happen, the child who would normally transfer will openly say to their carer, 'I know that you won't come up with me. I am angry and I will tell you when I can calm down.'

Sometimes a child may need to cause these whirlwinds – for example, they may have stolen money from their carer and understand that they will be in trouble when they get home from school. With a carer who is counter-transferring, all the child needs to do is to escalate the carer so that the carer cannot address the missing money, and once the whirlwinds are both up, the problem goes away (i.e., if everything ends in a shouting match, it is unlikely that the carer will return to the original problem of the child stealing some money).

Have a try at this with a child you are working with who has calmed after a challenge. Explain that you are thoughtful as to why you both end up in this difficult space, and own your role in it too. By starting at ground level, show the child what starts the whirlwind, how you responded, and then how they responded back, and as you explain, draw the whirlwinds charging each other to get bigger and bigger. Once you get to the top, explain how you are feeling and ask how the child might have felt. If you then explain that you are not happy that you lose your control, and from now on you will stay on the ground, that you will invite them to do the same, but it is okay, because it takes two to create the transference and counter-transference, this process is very much like Jessica's behaviour cycle (see '20. Cause and Effect Thinking'), but the difference is that the change comes from the carer, the adult as the person who doesn't follow the whirlwind upwards.

35

Thinking Cycle

This is a really good thinking process to assist children to explore how to manage thoughts and actions, but use it sparingly!

Wait for an opportunity to use this activity, and if done well, the child may learn to do this independently as they navigate relationships and responsibilities.

As an example of how this cycle works, let's imagine that a 13-year-old boy has been having difficulties with another peer at school; this peer has been name calling and bullying him. He tells you that he is going to go to school the next day and find the bully and punch him in the nose and beat him up. Our normal response might be to persuade him not to, to threaten, cajole, reason or plead. Thinking things through with the young person, following their train of thought, might prove helpful for the moment and for future cause and effect thinking.

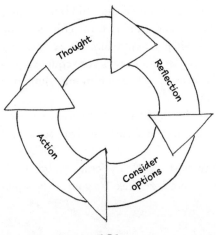

If we try not to shut down the intent but explore the thinking process, we might make a longitudinal difference rather than a potentially directed singular response. I would ask how he would go to school and hit the peer bully. I would bear witness to his plan and be thoughtful as to the potential of it. This is the first part of the cycle – thinking of an action.

The next part of the cycle is to reflect on the possible outcomes of the thought. This might include reflections of how, where, when, who and why, as well, of course, as the 'What are you wanting to achieve?' This, again, is helping the child to sequence, to visualize the potential impacts of the behaviour. I often choose to use the concept of a decision tree here (I talk about this as a separate communication skill in '38. Decision Trees').

I would ask the child what might happen if he did hit the child – what were the potential good things and what might be the bad things? He might feel justified that he hit the boy and felt good, but the teachers would find out and he might be in trouble. I might discuss the consequences of hitting a child, be those potential punishments from adults, being hurt by the child and/or his friends, getting into trouble with his carers, or having his freedom in the play space curtailed. And how might other people react? Especially those he has who are friends or important to him.

Then move the child to the next part of the cycle, by discussing the alternative actions that might meet the objective without hitting the child or getting into trouble. This should be done jointly with the child; you may suggest that the child speaks to his teacher and explains how angry he is about the child he wants to 'sort out'. He may suggest that the hitting of the child might have to happen after school, or that his friends could hit the child for him, or perhaps he might say that he will just ignore him. These options can then follow decision trees ('38. Decision Trees') or sequencing cause and effect thinking ('20. Cause and Effect Thinking') outcomes to see if they are a better option.

Finally, move the child to the last part of the cycle. Here we will find out the action that he decides on. Let's see a working example:

Thought: I'm going to get Henry because he got me suspended. When I get back to school next week, I'm going to beat him up!

Reflection: Are there other ways you can let Henry know you are angry with him?

Consider options: What are the consequences for the different options you have come up with for letting Henry know you are angry with him?

Action: What will you do now?

As with the many other tools discussed in this book, I would like to offer an example of practice.

I worked with a 15-year-old female who had endured horrible banter (bullying) over the whole term of her school. She struggled with her confidence and had low self-worth, but it had got to the point that her anger had overwhelmed her shame. She wanted to hurt.

She was in a meeting with me and her foster carer, and stated that she would get her own back when she went back to school after the holidays, and specifically she would hit the child who had caused her the most hurt. Instead of appealing to her, dissuading her, and at the worst, her carer warning her of the consequences, we drew the thinking cycle on her wallpaper. Then we walked through her thinking – so acknowledging her plan and what was driving her hurt. Once done, we then considered the consequences of the action she planned to take. What would happen? How would the child she hurt respond? Would others hurt her back? What might the school do? Would she get into trouble? Might her carers be told? All this thinking was written out on the wallpaper as it was discussed, and then we were able to work through rather than lecture through the challenges.

Then we moved to think about other ways we might act that would make sure that the next term may not be so challenging. To this we thought through telling the teacher of the previous term's experience; of avoiding the bullies; we thought of ways to deflect or manage the cruel things said to her; meeting with pastoral services, and so on. These other options were then considered for outcomes, and once completed (written on the wallpaper), the carer and I invited the young person to decide what action she wanted to take.

It may not surprise you, but she stated that she would still go and attack the child, but when the term started, she asked her carer to meet with her support teaching assistant at school and the situation was resolved. Mapping out thoughts through words and pictures is a great way to help children to see beyond the one-dimensional response that might be perceived as a threat, or dismissal.

What about a 15-year-old who is involved with a group of young people who are known to be engaged in criminal behaviour? She asks her carer if she can go out with her friends to the town centre and hang around. This request is either met with a 'yes' or 'no' response with a parental view of the situation. There is a wonderful opportunity for the child and the carer to work through the thinking cycle, or they could use cause and effect thinking (explored earlier in this book, in '20. Cause and Effect Thinking').

36

Good Things, Bad Things

This is a really simple but effective way of making sense of an action and whether it would be a good or bad idea; it also allows those involved to explore the reasoning and desires that might drive the need for the intention to be realized or for it to be withdrawn.

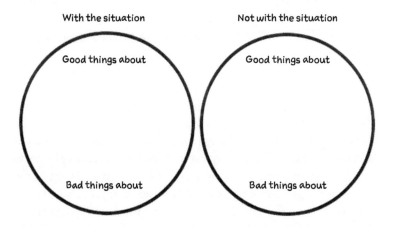

With the situation   Not with the situation

Good things about   Good things about

Bad things about   Bad things about

Look at the two circles here – the left circle is if you decide to do something and the consequence of doing this, and the right circle is the consequence of not doing something. Think about our 15-year-old and her request to go to town with her friends from '35. Thinking Cycle'.

    With one colour write the words at the top of the circle stating, 'Good things about going to town with my friends', and then, in the circle and in the same colour pen, encourage the child to write the good things. This might include 'having a laugh', 'catching up', 'might get some snacks', 'window shopping' and 'it's exciting'. Then, with another colour, write at the bottom of the circle the words 'Bad things about going to town with my friends', and in the same colour, write the bad things. These might include 'I might shoplift with them', 'we will get into trouble', 'I might end up in trouble again', 'I have no money' and 'you will be angry if I went'. Once completed, think through some of these good and bad things.

For some children, this is enough to show them the reasons for concern, and hopefully the balance between the two. For other children, a second circle is needed. In this second circle write the same at the top and bottom as the first. The emphasis now is what would be a good thing if the 15-year-old didn't go to town with her friends. Ask the child to consider the good things about not going and write them down in the colour of good things. These might include: 'I will be safe', 'I won't get into trouble', 'I can relax and do things at home' and 'it won't be an argument between me and my family'. Then, with the colour for bad things, the child might ask you to write what might be bad for her. This might include: 'I might lose their friendship', 'they might tease me', 'I will miss out on what they get up to' and 'they will think I am a goody two-shoes'.

Once this is done, there is a multitude of thoughts and feelings on the paper, and what was a request has now been explored, and both child and carer can bear witness to their positions. Not only does this help in decision-making; it also supports conversation, compromise and attentive attention. Although a lot of Egan listening skills are not so relevant when working with traumatized children, active listening is helped when that active ingredient of conversation is visual and co-created. Egan listening skills are a series of approaches to aid a listener to listen actively. Among the styles introduced by Egan is the acronym SOLER – SOLER instructs the counsellor to Sit squarely; to maintain an Open posture; to Lean towards the child; to maintain Eye contact and finally to Relax in the hope the child will copy. SOLER is the last thing you would want to do with a child or young person who may feel fear if any, some or all of these instructions were followed. As an example, if you sought eye contact with a child who felt that you could see their soul – it is hard to conceal true emotions with your eyes, they betray you, then this would feel similar to an attack, not as a connection. If you leaned towards a child, the invasion of their protective space might require a response or an unwelcome invitation (Egan 2002).

As Confucius (450 BCE) reportedly said, if you tell someone something, they will forget. If you show someone something, they might remember, but if you involve someone in something, they will understand. In this example of the child wanting to go to town with her friends, she can involve her carer in the thinking and the carer can do the same.

The joy of this activity is the infinite subjects you can explore, such as contact, school, family connection and being in care. In my therapeutic life story work I often have children who ask to do the circles to support decisions that they need to make, the last one being 'What do I do next – college, sixth form or apprenticeship?'

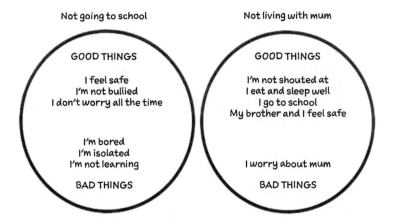

37

Magical Thinking Cycle

THE FACT, FICTION, FANTASY AND HEROISM TOOL

Over the last few years I have worked on the Fact, Fiction, Fantasy and Heroism tool (I developed this model in 2004), and it has become a commonly used tool, but after countless use, children and adults I have worked with have helped me shape it and modify it to be useful to practitioners to support their young people and children to talk about challenging things.

The magical thinking cycle is a very simple but effective short-burst activity that has proved to be a fantastic communication tool. It started as a Fact, Fiction, Fantasy and Heroism tool, and I would use this to help children to think about a part of their story, or some-one in their story, and so explore what they know, what they have been told, what they would do to make things easier and who can help. As an example, when thinking about myself – what is factual? I am married, have two sons and am 59. What is fiction? People say that I am very generous, that I would do anything for anyone if I could, that I work non-stop and am 'crazy'. What would I fantasize about in my life? To be happy, to make a positive difference to as many children and families as I can, to have a long life. Finally, who can help me? The children and families I work with, my family, and those who care about me.

The top-left quadrant captures the truth of something, but that truth is the author's understanding. If I was completing this on a typical 13-year-old I work with, I might write – 'challenging of others', 'experience of self-harm', 'dry humour' and 'clever'. Then in the bottom-left quadrant I would write what other people say about the child

– I might write 'angry', 'doesn't listen', 'will swear and be confronting' and 'ungrateful'.

Once done, we move to the top-right quadrant. This space is to look to hopes for the child, or wishes for objectives, and I might fill this quadrant with 'to like himself', 'to settle', 'to be likeable and attached' and 'to feel safe'. The final bottom-right quadrant is there to identify who might be able to support the child in the 'Hopes and wishes' quadrant and any other issues that may have been identified by the left quadrants.

Once complete, you have a magical thinking cycle that can now be used as a conversation tool – and it is brilliant. As an example, the subject to be thought through might be school – 'What is true about school?' 'What do people say about school?' 'What are your hopes and wishes for school? 'How can it be better for you?' And finally, 'Who can help you?' The most common themes I use are family members, faith, culture, friends and school, as they are so quick to do, and they deliver conversation and opportunities for change.

I have called it the magical thinking cycle as it provides the chance for anyone to think of a challenge or a person or an activity and high-light their understanding of it. Once completed, we can then discuss it without the interruptions or misinterpretations that often happen when we don't listen well.

This easy cycle is a great way of witnessing magical thinking and drawing out the current understanding of the internal and external world view of the author of the cycle on the subject raised. Please remember, though, that this is not just about people; it can be used to talk about certain events, themes and situations too.

Let us look at a worked example.

> The child is not seeing his older brothers (who were the people who sexually hurt him). He is struggling with the decision and misses them. They have been apart for over a year and he is worried that he might never see them again.
>
> True: 'I love my brothers', 'I miss them', 'They used to play with me and I don't have anyone to play with at the moment', 'They don't think about me any more'.
>
> Story: 'My brothers were naughty', 'My brothers are not safe', 'My brothers need to be helped to be good', 'My brothers are having help because they are getting angry', 'My brothers cannot be trusted as they get very angry with me'.
>
> Hopes and wishes: 'I want them to be safe', 'I want them to stop wanting to hurt me', 'I want to see them on my 18th birthday – I will be big enough then and can protect myself', 'I want to be able to be safe too'.
>
> Who can help? 'My brothers love me and they need to be helped by their carers to be safe with me', 'I need to learn to protect myself, so I could learn Kung Fu!', 'Social workers need to help me be safe when I see my brothers', 'They need a good mum to help them, like I have, but not the same, as my mum is my mum!'

This gives you an understanding of how the child sees their world. I have used this model in school challenges – going to school, lessons where there has been a loss of internal control. You might use this for torn loyalty, reviews, behaviour and wishes and feelings. In this drawing, Hazel has drawn her magical thinking cycle based on her dog!

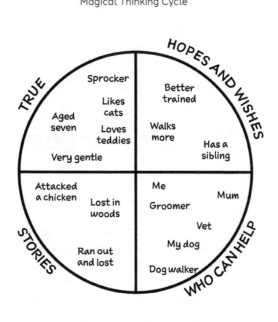

38

Decision Trees

Decision trees are very helpful to illustrate cause and effect, and then to encourage the opportunity of thinking. Unlike our previous discussion around cause and effect thinking ('20. Cause and Effect Thinking'), the decision tree is a multilinked process that can be followed ad infinitum. I worked with a nine-year-old child a few years ago and we spent a great deal of wallpaper time on her decision tree. It started with a simple question, 'Why can't I go home?' Of course, a simple but sometimes the hardest question of all for a child in the care system.

So we looked at a decision tree as a way of visualizing the questions that emanate from the first. Like many decision trees in computing, health decisions, assessments and executive strategy, a decision tree is binary, with two options. For my decision trees, I use a simple course of 'Yes' or 'No'.

Not only could my nine-year-old child see the different ways she could respond (the arrows pointing up mean 'Yes' and the arrows pointing down mean 'No'), she could see that the challenge of going home was not a simple 'Yes' or 'No' as there was then another node, another question with a simple 'Yes' or 'No', but the answer might lead to more difficult questions and eventually realization of what was possible and what was not, alongside the response that might inform rather than dismay the child and her original question.

Try it out, and for every question just give either a 'Yes' or 'No' answer; remember to think overtly about the possibilities and then follow the positive and negative routes. One of my young people completed the tree with me on her anger and how to manage it better, to see what she could do differently. Another young person used it with me to think about contact with her birth family through social media, and another on whether to go out with her friends, knowing that they were going to get drunk and take drugs.

39

Narrative Trees

Narrative trees are extremely useful tools to support the collation of information that you would not be able to achieve through question-and-answer-based interviews. I use narrative trees in the therapeutic life story work, court work and family assessments.

Think of the make-up of your family in three generations, and then draw out a genogram that is just the skeletal of your own tree. This is just the framework; do not add names or symbols at this point.

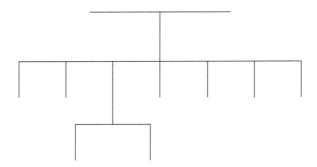

If I was to tell you that my mum is called Barbara and my dad is called Robin, what have I actually told you? I haven't had to think about it and they are just names. if I told you that my brothers and sisters are Mandy, Becky, Richard, Matthew, David, Lizzie, Kate, all I have told you is a bunch of names I have learned off by heart.

You won't know who is who, if any have died or moved away, yet family trees can be that one-dimensional. I introduced the concept of narrative trees in 1998 and I thoroughly recommend them to all social workers and care providers when doing family assessments and interventions.

How about you sort out your skeletal tree? Try and do a three-generation tree, so if you're a grandparent you would be at the top, your children in the middle and then your grandchildren at the bottom. Likewise, if you are a parent, you would be the middle, your children at the bottom and your parents at the top. Finally, if you do not have children, you would be at the bottom, your parents in the middle and your grandparents at the top. Just a space, remember – don't add names at this point.

Looking at my skeletal, I would now think of each person on my tree and try and think of something I could draw that would remind me of them. My hippocampus is filtering and preparing some memories for me to choose, and at the same time my hypothalamus and amygdala are deciding whether to protect, project or stay calm.

For my mother, I would draw some super moose, for my younger son a hockey stick, and so on and so on. Look at your skeletal tree and draw something that reminds you of the people in your family and then draw it where their name would normally sit. As you do this, you should have visualized pictures of these people and memories should be passing by.

Once there is a picture for each person, you are ready to share lives and share stories. By congregating around a story, we get to listen, to share and to become informed. For the children I work with, we do a skeletal of their tree and their carer's tree. We then take it in turns to talk about each picture on each tree and how it relates to us, and so we share a little that we might not normally.

As a communication tool, the information that gets discussed gives a more vibrant and real account of who the child is and how they fit or don't fit within a family, community or school.

> As a working example of a narrative tree, when a child and her long-term carer did a narrative tree each for me, the child wasn't on the carer's tree, but the whole of the child's family tree was her carer's family – she hadn't included any of her family of origin. Once we started telling the stories of the people on our trees, the body language, smiles and/or gritted teeth all gave an insight into the family-held narratives.

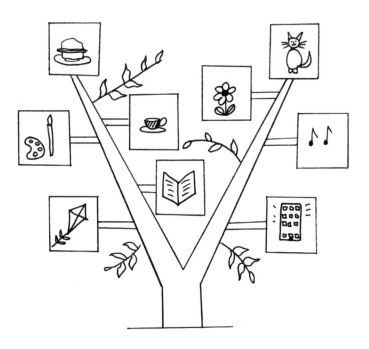

Try this out with your family or friends, and I am sure it will be a major intervention you will come back to use throughout the work in front of you. By the way, the super moose wasn't a hair product, it was a story about, well let's use four stones with a word on each – 'Food', 'Arguments', 'Pain', 'Anger' – and as it is my story, my fifth stone says 'Chocolate'. Using these story stones, I would have told you about my family, my mum, and a misunderstanding that could have caused more than a beating and the theft of two Pink Panther bars.

40

Timelines

Timelines help people make sense of where they are, where they have been, and what they have done or what they have been through in their life. They help to tell a journey of the life they have lived so far, from their perspective.

The child can tell you their story, or the child can tell you about an incident (e.g., the child has had a rocky fortnight). You could, for example, start with the child stating what happened that was good today, then what happened that was less good. Then map what happened yesterday, etc. Once the child has developed their timeline around the incident, you may want to have the child map a separate timeline for the person with whom the child has had an issue (to develop empathy and perspective-taking).

The timeline can vary – it can be a certain number of years, months or weeks, or it could be an entire lifespan. Whenever I have used a timeline, I have been amazed at how it can unlock many memories that are often suppressed or merely hard to retrieve. There is a technique to using a timeline, and when done well it can help provide insights into the child's world and how they have shaped their life to meet their needs (and wants). I would like you, the reader, to try this out as we go through the process, and in doing so, I hope that you will not only like it, but also use it in your day-to-day practice.

With a big piece of paper, using a colour pen draw a line down the middle of the paper. The line works well if it is drawn as a wavy line, or a river, a railway line or a road.

Then choose a time frame for this – why not put 'o' on the left side and your current age on the right – for me this will be 58! With timelines, the brain is like an onion, and so the multilayers are sequential. We need to start at the top and gently reveal the layers, so in the timeline we start at the here and now. Timelines are also done well when you have two main subjects to concentrate on. In my work I concentrate on home and work; with children it might be home and school, for example.

Using the timeline as a map, I would start with my age and write above my line, and where it says '58' identify where I live. I would then think about where I live, who I live with, what I like about it and what I don't. Sometimes I ask children to use a scale, on 1–10, with 1 being horrible and 10 being brilliant. Why don't you have a go? Where do you live, who lives with you and what do you think about this? Once done, I would then think about how long I have lived in the house I am in – for me this would be when I was 31, so I would travel left along my line and then about midway I would identify where I was living and the same questions and memories of those times will flood me.

If you are doing this, your mind should be reflecting and recalling on this moment in your life. If you carry on, your brain (hippocampus) starts to tune into your recall process and things start to upload to your conscious, quickly followed by emotions and visual impressions; maybe your other senses will be present. Carry on until you can't remember; you should get to the very early years and even remind yourself of where you were born. Don't forget to plot each of the memories along the line, and what you should find is the connections between each.

Once done, go back to your current age, as must I. In the now, and below the line, where do you work (or what are you now engaged in)? I would put 'TLSW' (therapeutic life story worker) as my employment, and then think about my work, what I like about it, the difficult and the challenging. I might even scale the job I have – for me it would be a 10. Have a go – where do you work? Do you go to school? College? Apprenticeship? Hobby? Retirement etc.? As with the home journey, go backwards and plot your work journey to university, college, school, nursery and even childminding. As you plot, write what you remember, what you are feeling, and allow yourself to dwell there for a few moments.

Once the two areas have been explored, go to being 'o' – who was in your family when you were born? Then plot the family as you move forward to the present day – who has joined, who has left? Each will provide a story and a communication. Finally, what about faith, culture and the things that are important to you? Some of the timelines I work with are over 2 metres long, and when done well, the stories, the trauma, the hurts and the fun, the good things and those long lost become tolerated and externalized, and recovery becomes more hopeful.

As for a working example, well, you have hopefully done your own as you read through this intervention!

41

Bronfenbrenner and the Solar System

Uri Bronfenbrenner was a well-respected Russian American theorist, and in 1977 he suggested that every child is surrounded by a nested structure of organization. He named these according to the proximity to the child, whereby the child is at the centre.

He pictured five concentric circles, from the first containing the child to the fifth ending with the chronosystem (the ordered and disordered history and future of the child). His work is well regarded as it acknowledges the interplay between the circles as they move away from the child. The five circles in order contain the child and all that is directly connected to the immediate environment of the child, then to the parents and neighbourhood. The next circle contains school, work and law and politics, followed by the next circle representing society, ideology and economy. The final circle influences the child, such as ageing, developing and moving through other phases of the concentric circles.

If, like me, you are a little confused by this, don't worry. The best thing that Bronfenbrenner ever 'may have said', although never published, is the often quoted, 'Every child needs at least one adult who is irrationally crazy about him or her'. If I was to have anything written about me, it would be something similar, that the secret of my work with hard-to-reach children is to be irrationally crazy about them – and I am, until I am usurped by their carer, which is, of course, my aim.

In this activity I have used Bronfenbrenner's bioecological theory to design my approach to understanding a child's world. I use the solar system as a model of enquiry and discovery. This diagram can be used to map who is involved in the child or young person's life, and how they feel about the involvement of that person or service. I often refer to this as a child's solar system – they are the Sun and everything revolves around them; they are the centre of their universe.

The next layer to add names to is the friendly planets. The third layer is the dangerous region, where the asteroids live – here, I invite children to add any names of people in their lives who worry, scare or have hurt them. Finally, the outer ring is the place we put the names of people who are involved in a child's life who are there to help, and outside the solar system are people who are no longer involved.

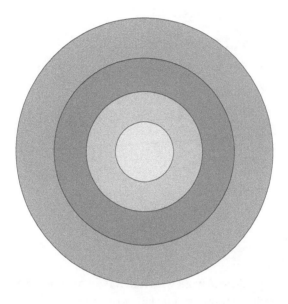

This activity provides a check-in with the child, and this can be revisited over the time of the intervention you are engaged with. It can also be used to show how life changes as people and events appear and disappear. It gives the child or young person a voice, and they are able to demonstrate who is important to them, who they have in their life and who they maybe don't want to see. It also allows them to understand why certain people are in their life and others are not, thus allowing for more open discussions.

Let us look at a worked example.

Our individual's name is Tom. He is the Sun, and everything surrounds him, just like our worlds. The people important to Tom include Sally, Mike and JJ, his carers and younger brother. The people Tom doesn't want in his world, who worry and/or scare him, are his dad and grandad. The people he doesn't really want in his life, but they have to be, are his social worker, therapist and support worker. In the world of his yesterday, he has the judge who decided he had to be in care, and previous carers he misses.

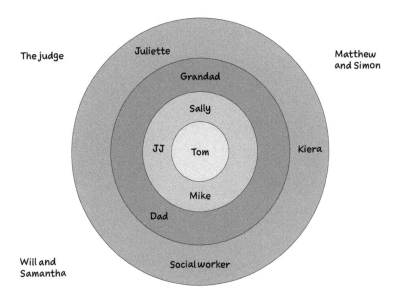

A few of my children I work with find it hard to understand things in one-dimensional terms, so I make a solar system with them. We use ping-pong balls, pipe cleaners and paint. We colour the balls yellow, green, red and brown; for the outer space we use black or blue ping-pong balls. This way we create the child's universe and write names on the balls for the relationship they offer. A good thing with this visual process is that we can change the colour of the relational ball, so if the child feels that their grandad is a good person, we can move the grandad from red to green. This helps when children have understood their connection was not okay, but when thinking about this person and what they did or do, they may feel the person did their best. Social workers and foster carers often move from brown to green as understanding occurs.

It is helpful to use this approach when thinking about school, care and family – we are all connected, and once the solar system is complete, the narrative of the family, school and neighbourhood can be explored and understood. For some children we might just draw a universe of emotions and identify a colour planet for each emotion and a memory for each.

42

What, Why, When, How, Where and Who

Rudyard Kipling is the author of such things as *The Jungle Book* and *Mandalay* as well as poems and stories contained in his *Just So Stories*, and one of his poems has shaped my practice:

I keep six honest serving men
(They taught me all I knew);
Their names are What and Why and When
And How and Where and Who.

I send them over land and sea,
I send them east and west;
But after they have worked for me,
I give them all a rest

I let them rest from nine till five,
For I am busy then,
As well as breakfast, lunch, and tea,
For they are hungry men.
But different folk have different views;
I know a person small –
She keeps ten million serving men,
Who get no rest at all!

She sends 'em abroad on her own affairs,
From the second she opens her eyes –
One million Hows, two million Wheres,
And seven million Whys! (Kipling 1902)

Writing in 1902, Kipling explains childhood curiosity, and for me this provides a perfect structure for helping a child make sense of their internal, relational and external world. My interpretation of this story in this format is that the 'person small', a child, has experienced an unsettling incident, and curiosity becomes a preoccupation leading to another famous poem by Kipling, 'If'.

Communicating with children will involve a process of asking questions that lead with the five 'w's and one 'h'. We are often asked 'why?' when a better start might be 'what?' Or maybe another important 'w' – 'wonder'? In this activity, we use the concept of curiosity to picture the whole story and pay respect to each angle.

There has been an incident that needs to be understood, so the first thing to say is 'My job is not to tell you off; you have many people in your life to do that. It is my job to help you to work out what went wrong and what we might be able to do about it'.

To assist you with this tool, think of a time when something hadn't happened in the way you intended – perhaps a family discussion, a domestic disagreement or maybe a task at work that didn't!

The first step is to ask yourself *what* happened? Look for a narrative from the earliest connection and follow your story forward to the end of the incident. This free narrative without intervention will set the scene. In reality, done well, you are dissecting the incident and creating a clearer understanding of exactly what occurred. We are, in effect, asking for a description, a narrative, often to picture the event for the listener.

The second stage is *why* – 'why' is often regarded as a blaming question, justifying an action, and it is the 'why' question that I change to 'wonder'. I wonder what the reason was for this happening? I wonder about the choices that were made? I wonder what you think about that? We are, in effect, looking for reason.

Then we can think of timing, at what juncture the event happened. It could be a time, an order of events to help centre the communication to a period that makes sense to us. We are, in effect, looking for a time, a *when*.

Following timing, we move to the question of *how*? This is a descriptive question, to ascertain the systemic process of an event and the meaning of its process. *How* allows a narrative of explanation of the workings of an event from the voyeur's understanding, and helps to make sense of the event and the outcome. We are, in effect, looking for the process and actions.

I am hoping that you can see Kipling's clever words – to truly understand something, it is not simply to ask one question, but to be curious of all angles of interest. The next question is the location, *where* the event happened. The *where* allows us a geographical concept – was it at school, home, a friend's house or in the park? We are, in effect, looking for the environment and how it plays into the event.

Finally, we are at the last of the six, the *who*? The actors involved in the event can be crucial in making sense of something that may have occurred. This question will provide the interested parties with the details of others present, and the protagonists, the bystanders and those who may have tried to help. The *who* allows context of others, witnesses, perpetrators, friends and maybe foes. We are, in effect, looking for others to talk to, to blame, to place responsibility on, or acknowledge vulnerability.

When interviewing, completing court reports, therapeutic work and assessments, this model and the process is an invaluable communication tool. Once the five 'w's and one 'h' are completed, you can ask the child or young person how they feel about the incident. You might find it helpful to ask at each 'w' or 'h' how they feel, exploring with the child or young person what they could have done differently. Discuss the options that open up at each level and why those actions might have led to a different outcome.

> As a working example, you are working with a child who has had a difficult contact with her birth family. During the contact the child and birth parent disagreed on something – let's suggest a PlayStation game where tea is ready but the child won't stop the game or turn the game off or on pause. This leads to an argument between the child and her mother, and in frustration, the child punches the wall and damages the wall and her fingers.

As the worker for the child, you see the bandaged hand and the support for her broken fingers and comment as to how she has been hurt. By asking the questions above in the systemic way that is shown, you would get a full story (from the child's perspective) of the event. You will get to understand what happened, to work out the reasons, the people involved, the time it happened, the process, and finally, who was involved.

43

Memory Jars and Boxes

This activity is helpful for children to express a variety of memories by using jars of coloured sand, salt or beads. Each colour represents an emotion for that memory. Memory jars are used in therapeutic work all over the world. Many variations can be found on the internet, and different organizations also have their own versions.

One way a memory jar is often used is in grief and loss work; indeed, my mother has a memory jar for my dad. When he died, we wanted to capture the memories of him from as many people as we could. At his memorial event, as he had sadly died during Covid-19, we couldn't have a full funeral. So, when it was safe, all those connected to him came to a memorial service and each left a written memory on a colour Post-it® note to reflect that memory, and in the same colour they chose to write on, they put a small amount of sand in the jar. Three years on, the jar is at my mum's house, and I hope that it gives her comfort.

The best time to introduce a memory jar would be after several sessions of getting to know you, where hopefully mutual trust has been established. To set the task, I always try to explain that memories can be really good for us, but sometimes our brains get so full, and that there is little room for everything. Suggesting a memory jar to hold those important memories outside our brains would be a good thing for our brains to have a rest. It is a good thing to keep our memories safe and to be able to think and talk about them when we need to.

You need to get a jar, preferably a large jar with a screw-top lid. Then, acquire some cling film, an elastic band, some table salt, coloured chalk sticks and corresponding coloured Post-it® notes. With all these to hand, invite the child to do some work around memories. Ask them to choose colours to reflect emotions, say blue for sad, green for happy, yellow for excited and red for angry, and then perhaps pink for loving memories and orange for sad. Then get hold of a saucer, or a chopping board, and separately, for each chalk, grind the stick to dust. Once done, pour table salt into a bowl and add the grounded chalk to it.

The salt will change colour to the chalk colour added, and now you have coloured salt – you can, of course, buy coloured sand, but you don't need to spend more than is needed. For each coloured chalk stick, mix with 200g of salt and you will end up with salt chalk; if you get six bowls or container tubes these can be kept in a tidy and secure way.

With the coloured Post-it® notes, ask the child to think of a memory and the colour of the emotion the memory sits with. When ready, write the memory on the coloured Post-it® note.

When concluded and thought through, invite the child to pour in a little of the coloured sand that fits the Post-it® note colour (about 2mm depth would be fine). For each session I would suggest that you do five of these Post-it® notes, as it can prove overwhelming for some if you do too many. Try and include a range of emotions and memories such as 'happy', 'sad', 'angry', 'loving' or 'excited', or you might be more direct and ask the child if they have any sad memories, and so on.

As each memory is acknowledged and validated, the jar will have five important memories after the first session and perhaps two centimetres of different-coloured sand. As an example, a social worker is working with a child who is struggling with a recent change of family and she is missing her siblings. The successive Post-it® notes at the end of each session are placed in the upside-down jar lid; cling film is placed on top of the opened jar to seal in the coloured salt, which, by now, will feel more important as representing the physical memory.

Then, with rubber bands, secure the cling film in place and carefully screw the lid on – you have helped to make a memory jar. The Post-it® notes don't fall through to the coloured salt as the cling film keeps them safe in the upturned lid. If you find that the jar is full, then you could start a second one, which is bigger, and transfer what is in the first to the second.

You do not need a jar for this work; you could draw a box on paper – as big as you can make it – and then write the child's name on the front with 'memory box' next to the name. Then invite the child to put in all the memories that they would like to share and fill the box; it is good to offer to write for the child as they can then concentrate on their memories. It is often the case that the box is quickly filled, and children have more to say. I remind them that I cannot give them another brain, so we will need to write over what is already there.

As you write over the top of the previous memories, the child and their carer will start to see how confused and mixed up memories can get. This is the perfect opportunity to suggest that talking about the memories and making sense of them might mean they take less space as we declutter the brain and so help the child to be less preoccupied.

When I introduce memory jars to children, they often choose not to do them, but they do seem to like the box drawing, and others are more creative. Some of the children I have worked with use computer games such as Minecraft™, LEGO® or other building blocks. In Minecraft™, some of the children like to build a brain village that can hold their memories, wishes and hopes. We can use LEGO® Fortnite or LEGO® to build houses to hold different types of memories and different people who have lived in various houses and various families. We can choose the pens we work with to match the colour for each emotion experienced when thinking about the memory or being experienced as we talk about it.

I have found that this memory approach can lead to a more proactive and therapeutic opportunity to support a person to remember and externalize their past and, once understood, they are able to make their peace with the trauma and the past no longer holds their present.

44

Mirror Work

Reflection is a major aim of communicating with children, and using a reflective surface is a great way of doing this activity. I have found this extremely useful when working with younger children and children with learning challenges.

You can use real mirrors, but I have found it more helpful to make one.

Using a large piece of aluminium cooking foil, about the size of a foolscap A4 page, stick this to a larger piece of paper and then invite the child to draw a frame around the edges of the foil. This activity will produce a framed mirror, but the idea is that the foil is not crystal clear, but a little blurry. The mirror can then be used to see a reflection of the past, the reality of the present, or the hope for the future.

I use the mirror to encourage the child to explore what their future self might be like, to reflect on a family member or someone they miss or are fearful of. I also do letters to the future and letters from the past, using the mirror as a thinking 'anchor' point.

As an example, you could ask the child, who might be 10 years old, 'Look in the mirror and describe what you notice if you could see your 20-year-old "self"'. Following this, you could ask about clothes that were worn, the background, whether there were others with their older self, where they were living, and so on.

Sometimes when I work with children about their trauma past, I use mirror work to separate the child from the event. As with air balloons (introduced earlier in this book, see '13. Air Balloon') it distances the child from the actual event, and provides a barrier that can be seen as protection. This step back can be enough to talk about the most difficult of memories and worries, and once done, the mirror could be used for fun discussions – 'If this was your birthday party that you can see in the mirror, who would be there? What presents would you have, and what is the best thing about your birthday?'

45

Then and Now

One of the things I often find when working with children and carers is the impact of caring on the carer themself. It is also true that carers, be they birth family, connected, foster or adopting, are often the last to see change in the children they care for.

For those of us fortunate enough to work with families, we do see the changes far more easily, especially if we visit families once every two weeks. If we then add the hurt, traumatized and angry child who seems to be just this, day in and day out, the vicarious trauma of this also plays its hand. It is often at this juncture that I use a 'Then and Now' chart – similar to the one shown here, and based, once more, on a number of different cases. After working with a 14-year-old girl and her foster mother, the foster mother suddenly announced that she had done nothing to make a difference to the child since she had come to live with her. The child asked if she could do something on the wallpaper, and with agreement, she drew a large square and drew a line down the middle. On the left-hand side she wrote the word 'Then' and on the right-hand side she wrote 'Now'.

In the left-hand column, she drew a picture of two people fighting and a smaller person being hit by one of the fists of the taller drawn figure. Then she drew a picture of drug syringes and sharp knives, a picture of cigarettes, and then some clothes with holes in. Finally, she drew a very dirty bath and a large bin with a lid on. Once done, she explained to her carer,

> When I lived with my parents they would often fight and hurt each other. Sometimes I would get hurt too. There were lots of drugs and dangerous things in my home and people would always be smoking. My clothes were old and smelly and we never had baths; you can see

that the bath is dirty. I drew the bin because there was never any food at home so we would see what was in the bins outside.

Then she drew in the right-hand column a picture of people arguing, a clean bath, nice clothes, a box for all the knives, a cigarette picture crossed out and finally, lots of food and chocolate on plates. Once finished, she told her carer,

> I have lived with you for six years, and we argue, but we don't hurt each other and we are always okay afterwards. All the sharp and dangerous things are locked up and safe; I have clothes that I get to choose and they are not old and worn by others. We have good food, healthy food, and I don't have to worry about being clean as we have the cleanest bath in the world. No one takes drugs, you are not even allowed to smoke or swear in this house – I am safe!

Imagine, all of you reading this, reflecting on your children – you make the difference even if you sometimes cannot see it. A reminder may make all the difference as the heavy load of caring for hurt children is difficult enough. You can do the 'Then and Now' on subjects such as school change, placement change, contact and, of course, after trauma interventions such as Dyadic Developmental Psychotherapy, therapeutic life story work and other therapeutic interventions.

Then	Now

46

Hula Hoops

DRAMA WORK AND RE-ENACTMENT

Hula hoops are great ways to have opportunities to communicate challenging issues with children around trauma issues, bullying and worries. Based loosely on Gestalt's Empty Chair exercise, we can imagine the views and/or actions of someone or others in a safe environment. The Empty Chair exercise is a therapeutic practice within Gestalt therapy, where someone can engage in a conversation with an absent other, as if they were seated on a chair in the same room. Gestalt suggests, and I agree, that this conversation can lead to the resolution of internal conflict and unfinished business (Perls 1973).

You don't have to use actual hula hoops; string or ribbon – even a circle of sand or stones – will work as long as the circle is unbroken. I use hula hoops as they are solid rings and will maintain a sturdy containing space. With three hula hoops placed on the floor, I label them as certain people or groups of people. To explain this further, I have amalgamated another group of children I have worked with to create a case study.

I once worked with a 14-year-old girl who was struggling with questions that she wanted to ask her father. She hadn't been able to do this as she had been adopted from the age of four after being sexually abused by him.

These questions had been swirling around in her head and heart for many years and, due to the trauma and the confusions that had impacted her in her own behaviour and low sense of self, she would answer these questions with surety that all that had happened was her fault. I was working around her story and she asked me if she could write down her questions for her dad on the wallpaper, as she never wanted her dad to know she was still thinking of him.

I brought the hula hoops in the house and laid them on the floor in the front room. I explained that the red hoop was this girl, let's call her Raza. I then explained that the green hoop was her father and the blue hoop was me. Raza was then told that if any of us stood in a hoop, we would pretend to be that person, but if we stepped out of the hoop, then we were who we really are. We had a play, and I stood in the red hoop. As soon as I was there, I told everyone that I was Raza, and when I asked the father and Raza who I was, they both said I was Raza. I stepped out of the red hoop and was Richard again. Raza stood in the green hula hoop and she told me she was Richard, and again we all said, 'Hello'.

Once sorted, I then asked Raza to stand in her hula hoop, and I stood in her father's hula hoop. Raza's carer, let's call her Sara, then stood in my hula hoop. I then said, 'Raza, it's your dad here – I understand that you have some questions for me?' Raza replied with 'Were you or anyone in your family hurt physically or sexually?' Now, I can't answer for her father, and even if I did know, I wouldn't try to answer. I turned to 'Richard' in the green hoop and said, 'Richard, are you writing this question down? It is so important that I can think about the answer' and then 'Richard' (Sara) wrote the original question down. I then said to Raza, 'I am sorry, I need to really think about this. Do you have any other questions?' Raza asked four more questions and for each, her father asked 'Richard' to write them down.

We then stopped as I stepped out of the hula hoop and as Richard invited everyone else to do the same. We had a break and played a game for about 10 minutes and then returned to the hula hoops. This time I asked Raza to stand in the blue hoop, which was her father, I asked Sara to stand back in the green hoop, as Richard, and I stood in the red hoop, which was Raza.

As 'Raza', I said, 'Hi Dad, I have some questions for you. Richard, can you let me have those questions I wanted to ask Dad?' With the questions from 'Richard', I then asked 'Dad' (Raza) each one and with each one asked she responded with her thoughts. On each occasion I, as Raza, asked 'Richard' (Sara) to write the answers down next to the questions. Once done, I stepped out of the hula hoop, and as Richard, I invited everyone else to step out too.

Imagine – all the questions and answers that had been whirling around in Raza's head were now externalized and the information shared could now be thought through. It is a wonderful way to talk about the impossible and hard-to-face worries, and the outcomes have been remarkable.

I have used the same process for children who are being bullied. The red hula hoop is the child I am working with, the blue hula hoop would be the bully/ies, and the green hula hoop would be the teacher. Playing out the parts by allowing the child to be themselves or the teacher, to be the bullies, and then giving me the chance to play the same, we can work out ways to cope with and even manage the bullies.

As an example, one 10-year-old learned to respond to his bullies by calmly repeating, 'It is none of your business'. For older children, we can use the hula hoops to practise meetings and contact – for one 17-year-old child, who was in trouble for behaviour at college, we practised the college meeting – one hula hoop as the child, one hula hoop as the school principal and the other hoop as the student counsellor. After several try-outs the child attended her meeting and kept her head, apologized for her behaviour, and secured her long-term place in the college.

The next time that you have a child who has a challenge at school, get those hula hoops out and role-play the episode – the information you gain, conversation and potential next steps may prove invaluable.

47

Okay, Not Okay Book and Scrolls

Many children I meet have very sad experiences in their early lives and find it difficult to talk about them. If this was not challenging enough, for a few of these children, they are threatened by those who have hurt them that if they do talk about them, they will be hurt further. Some children are told that they might be in big trouble, that the police will arrest them, or even worse, that they will be blamed as it was their fault really.

Not everyone will like, or even agree with, this intervention, but I have found it most useful when working with children who state, 'I can't tell you' or 'I will be in trouble'. The saddest one I heard was from a 16-year-old who told me that her parents could see her through a magic mirror so they would always know. I use an Okay, Not Okay book – this encourages the child to write on the left page all the things that are okay to talk about and on the right page all the things that are not okay to talk about.

My experience is that, as long as you honour the lists made and ask only about the left page, but do not ask or do anything about the right page, the child will feel safe. Within two sessions children will normally say to me, 'It is okay, we can talk about that stuff under "Not okay", nothing happened when I told you things and so I guess I am safe'.

You can use scrolls in the same way, inviting the child to fill one scroll with questions and another with worries. The worry scroll can then be tied together with a ribbon and 'No access unless I am ready' signed by the child. Be patient and all will be revealed, as the child feels safer and assured by your ability to hold their pain and fear.

48

All About Me Books

*We are what we were; once we understand this, we have the oppor-
tunity to aspire to all we want to be.*

ROSE (2017)

This is such a brilliant communication tool, that if done every six
months, as soon as a child enters the care of a social care department,
or a child in need where the need might be as a result of disability,
becomes a story of the child. I am honoured by the number of agen-
cies, departments and social care organizations that have decided to
provide this for children and young people. Over the last four years I
have been involved in this approach, under the Rose Model of Therapeutic Life Story Work.[1] All About Me is designed to capture the child's
own story of their world as a snapshot of the 'now'.

In the USA, the Oregon Department of Human Services and
Oregon Post Adoption Resource Center have successfully integrated
this model to now offer a service to all the children in out of home
care, and now those children's carers are doing their own as well. In
the Northeast, Blue Cabin, ably led by Jenny Young,[2] and Darlington,
Gateshead and South Tyneside have integrated All About Me as a
direct intervention.

Utilizing the skills of artists, Blue Cabin developed Creative All
About Me[3] for groups of children. In Australia, MacKillop Family

1   See https://tlswi.com/about-tlswi
2   https://wearebluecabin.com/people/jenny-young
3   https://creativelifestorywork.com/about/what-is-all-about-me

Services[4] and Berry Street have initiated All About Me books for all children in their care (hundreds of young people); Settlement Services International in Sydney[5] have been using All About Me for four years, ably led by Ghassan Noujaim, a quite remarkable care professional and completely dedicated to the families and children he works for.

In the UK, we have many authorities using All About Me, and in 2024 both Cornwall and the Scottish Highlands will join the ever-increasing number of authorities seeing the potential that keeps a child's history and also invites communication by sharing lives and sharing stories.

Essentially, All About Me is a tool to help carers/support workers/ social workers to record a six-monthly snapshot of your child or young person's life, interests, achievements and thoughts. As the years go by, it is hopeful that a six-monthly update of the book can keep the information safe and up to date. If a child has been looked after for five years, they would have a collection of these snapshots, and when put together, this would create a 200-page document capturing their development, their interests, their achievements and their life journey so far. All About Me invites conversations with children and young people, to help them to keep information together about their life journey. This also promotes a sharing of life and the stories become a passport for the next adventure. For the adult supporting the completion of these All About Me books, time is available for the adult and child to actively build in potential attachment, emotional connection and attunement.

Children and young people gain a sense of their identity when they understand their history and background, including events and details about their parents' background and circumstances. All About Me assists you to have conversations with the child or young person about their current circumstances and how they see themselves, their carers and the world. In doing so, this reflection will help them connect to the past, and importantly, help them think about and plan for their future.

This tool explanation is lengthy, but it will help you use All About Me in a way that is meaningful for the child or young person and for those meeting their needs. Remember, the process is the child or

4   www.mackillop.org.au/about-mackillop/publications/the-case-for-early-intervention-in-victoria
5   www.ssi.org.au

young person's resource. It's their story, and not your story of them. Your role, whether as a practitioner or as a carer, is to help the child collect memories, stories and information, and to encourage the development of their stories. It provides a structure for collecting and storing the information, but uniquely grows with the child, and ultimately, if a child was to come into the care of the authority at two years of age and leave at 21, they would have 38 snapshots of their journey. In volume, 760 mostly self-written and co-created at times. That would be 760 pages charting their world, who has acted in their lives and the 'what', 'why', 'where', 'when', 'who' and 'how' of those events.

Imagine if you could pick up a personalized series of books of your life, charting your journey, interests and such. You would be curious as to whether you had friends at age six and what your favourite food was; you could try and remember; you might ask your parent or siblings. If you are in care, you might not have these resources to go to, but if you can collate and just read, in your own words, all about these things and more besides, it grounds you and provides clarity to what you come to believe.

When children and young people are subject to intervention from social services, it can be a confusing and anxious time. As decisions are made around the child or young person, the impact of these decisions will undoubtedly impact on the child. It is important for those involved in their life to help them keep records of their life's journey.

Life story work can be in any form that suits the child or young person. It is their personal record of their history, their life from before they were born, their birth, their present and the opportunity to look to the future. It can include anything that helps them understand why they are receiving support from others, and in turn, how they will be supported to understand their current circumstances.

For many children and young people, life story work helps their healing journey by understanding the present, revising the past and preparing them to experience a positive future. It is important that we hold dear the belief that children and young people are supported to learn about and maintain a connection to their culture – their family's ethnicity, religion/s and language/s – in this way, they will have better opportunities to stay connected with their family, culture and community. In time, this can contribute to positively shaping their self-identity and self-esteem, and future-proof their journey through adulthood.

Focusing on the journey of the child or young person's life story through a series of All About Me books provides an opportunity for you to have conversations with your child or young person and other significant people who have been or are related to the child or young person's life, including their family, social, education and health connections. Through these conversations, you may assist the development of a positive sense of self, of their identity, belonging and those around them who seek to support them.

Having completed the All About Me books in the hundreds, I have found the process supports the following for all those involved:

- It gives details and understanding of a child or young person's current view.
- It enables conversations with the child or young person to share realistic information about their past, current and future.
- It links the past to the present.
- It helps the child or young person connect and understand how early negative experiences may continue to affect them.
- It acknowledges separations and losses, and the impact of their past.
- It builds a sense of connection with family or community who may have been lost.
- It builds a sense of identity.
- It enhances self-esteem and self-worth.
- It enables the child or young person to develop a sense of security.
- It helps build relationships.
- It celebrates the child or young person's life.

For me, of all these advantages, the key elements are the potential to build a sense of self, identity and a safer working model. It is also the opportunity to build relationships, securing trust and security. The process has evolved and the All About Me book can benefit not just the child, but also the team around them – some local authorities have linked the process to their six-month statutory reviews and their fostering panel reviews.

When completing the All About Me book template (and by all means alter the template to meet the age and interests of the child), provide positive engagement and positive interest. Bring your curiosity so that the child can immerse themself in your engagement to tell their stories and be heard. You may find that some children need your permission to talk about things that they may have been discouraged to talk of previously. I often find reflective questions are useful, and this might give opportunities to develop or introduce new thinking.

When I complete All About Me books with children, I tend to complete two stages over three visits; this helps me to invite the child to talk about things the next time I come. All About Me books will provide a strong, continuous flow as the child completes the task every six months; as they do this, the carer or support worker will weave connections between the child or young person's present and past and into the future.

All children and young people are unique, and so your use of the process needs to capture the difference and celebrate the child. It is important to consider the child or young person's development, age and interests in the approach you take initially to start the conversation. On an ongoing basis, be guided by the child or young person as to what they want to focus on. The key thing to remember is that you are getting to know the individual, and you are helping them to collate information about their life.

To get the best out of the process, complete your own All About Me book (you can download a typical All About Me template from www.jkp.com/catalogue/book/9781805012900). Although I suggest key sections or topics, there should be no order as such, but all topics should be addressed. In Australia and in the West Coast of the USA, we concentrate on diversity and culture, and it is my hope that all books across the world will have culture at the centre.

This is me

This section is an opportunity to talk about the present and record favourite things that the child has at that particular time. It includes a range of prompts, such as:

- Favourite food
- Favourite music or song

- Favourite band or singer
- Favourite sport, game or toy
- Favourite colour/s
- Favourite animal/s
- Favourite book/s
- Favourite movie/s
- Favourite TV show or online program
- Favourite place
- Names of best friend/s
- One thing they like to do generally or on the weekend.

Try to ensure that the book collates information about the child that comes from them, and not from you. You might want to use the activities in this book to make the process fun. As an example, I would use the questions on the Jenga® blocks or the dominos/arches (see '5. Blocks' and '6. Jenga®'). Use all or some prompts and add others that are of interest for the child.

The All About Me book is there to acknowledge the child's interests, the things that give them joy, success and achievement as well as curiosity. Encourage the child to choose a picture or even draw a picture of themself; many of my children use avatars, other skins and other characters from Roblox™, Minecraft™, Pokémon™, and so on.

My family

Some children find talking about their family of origin as a request too far if they don't currently live within their family or extended family. This 'My family' section does not have to be their birth family; it might be their carer in the present or a past or hopeful future family. In each instance, that is fine. Be mindful; don't have a page that says, 'My father is...' if you know the child does not know their father. I often use starters like 'The people who look after me are...' or 'Other important people to me are...'

This section provides an opportunity to include details of the individual's parents, extended family members, siblings and other significant individuals, whether this be blended, confused or seemingly inaccurate.

If you can be patient and not corrective at the beginning, you can refocus the child at the end to confirm and accept what the child wishes to be in their book. Where possible, ask the child or young person's family members to provide information and pictures. Invite the child to draw a picture of the family member if photographs are not available. You could help them look into what the meaning of their family member's name may be as part of the life story work or in this process.

A family tree diagram can be included, and also, a 'Those who are important to me' diagram. This can then be discussed, and if you encourage debate, this will allow celebration and understanding of how the child or young person sees themselves in the family and community. It may be that a traditional tree is not helpful, so be creative and be involved.

Other information that may be of interest to include could be:

- Where did their parents and/or family grow up?
- Which school did their parents attend?
- What are the birth dates or death dates of significant family members?
- Where have the family gone for holidays?
- Who are the family's special friends?
- Do the family have pets?

Culture and identity: who am I?

It is important to provide an opportunity to add information about the individual's family background, including details about their parents and extended family's place of birth, traditions, rituals, faith practices, customs and language/s.

Consider the following questions to help you understand the individual's family's cultural influences, language(s), religion, and their involvement in community, cultural and religious activities:

- What language/s is spoken at home?
- What culture and/or religion does the family identify with?
- How does the family practise their culture and/or religion?
- What cultural or religious activities is the family involved in?
- Does the family have contact with members of their cultural community?

If so, is there information on:

- The cultural activities they like to be involved in?
- Whether the child or young person has contact with people from their cultural community?
- Whether they want to maintain or learn their first language?
- Whether they want to practise their religion?
- Whether the child or young person has a religiously prescribed diet?

Depending on the information available, the child might be interested in their mother and father's narrative, language, identity, faith and heritage. The same can be said about siblings and their relationship to the child as well as their connection. All About Me allows for a narrative about what the child or young person knows about their heritage and identity, and what they know about their place of origin, language(s) their family has used and/or faith they have practised.

For new-born children to toddlers: How often does the child hear stories and/or songs and/or listens to cultural music and/or attends cultural gatherings or ceremonies?

For children three years onwards: Consider whether the child participates and practises cultural activities and/or takes part in ceremonies related to faith and/or festivals and events, such as art and craft and/or is exposed to culturally related dress or listens to culturally specific music, dance and/or eat cultural food.

For young people about 13 years and older: Consider whether the young person takes part in festivals and events, art and craft activities, or dresses, listens to cultural music and how they talk about their culture. The history of the family's country provides an opportunity to talk about the history of the child or young person's country of origin. If you are not abreast of details, do some research, find information and/or talk to a bilingual case worker, or find community leaders or ethnic services that may have relevant information.

Thinking of the traditional foods of the child's heritage allows for a conversation on what foods are common to the child or young person's family, what may be cooked on special events or on particular days or were common to the family.

My feelings

Emotional intelligence and the ability to realize emotions is an important part of who we are, and this section should provide an overview of feelings to help the child or young person use words to connect to their emotions. There are opportunities to encourage the individual to express different feelings and what may trigger these feelings. There are pages allocated for:

- 'I am happy when...'
- 'I am sad when...'
- 'I am angry when...'
- 'I am excited when...'
- 'I am scared when...'

My home

This section should provide an opportunity to record details of the child or young person's placement with the people who have care of them. Talk with the child or young person about their experiences of living where they do, and if applicable, memories of the places that they used to live in. Photographs are helpful in this section.

My school/nursery/college days

Remember to capture and reflect on the names of those involved in the education of your child or young person as well as an opportunity to secure those memories of childcare and preschool, primary school and senior school years. The prompt questions relate to memories, things the child or young person liked, their friends' names, memories of favourite things including how they remember themselves at that stage, and the things they were good at during that stage. You may like to start off with the present school year but you can go back afterwards to think about previous years with the child or young person, if they would like to.

My future

This section is the final session, and it is designed to encourage the child to record what they may be thinking about with regard to their future, including what they would like to be, and wishes for their future. The mirror tool ('44. Mirror Work') is very useful here.

Things I may need to know when I'm older

All About Me provides an opportunity to save special memories, records, certificates, reports etc. of things that the child or young person may be interested in or need when they are older. It might be helpful to add plastic sleeves to the folder to hold the memorabilia. Duplicate pages of specific sections such as 'This is me' are added to the back of the book to allow for multiple entries. Alternatively, you may use blank A4 paper and slot these into the folder provided.

Once completed, the template book is collected by the carer or social worker and a finished book is completed by using a programme such as PowerPoint or Book Creator. The book is then given to your child to approve, and as long as it captures the child's current understanding of their world and those within it, it becomes the new template for the next book to be updated in six months. The child, with the help of those around them, develops a journal of self, and when they leave care, they have their stories with them.

How do children use their book?

This depends on the child or young person's development and views. The book is a tool to help keep information together about their life that they may want to refer to as they are living in situations that require support from the council, for example, or when they are an adult and want to reflect on their history. But if they don't want to use the book, it's okay not to push them. Talk to them about how they want to keep their memories, or offer some other alternatives such as a treasure box or a scrapbook or photograph or video library.

If the child doesn't want to use the book, talk with them about whether you may use it to store some information about them as they are growing up, so they can look at it at a later stage. It is important that you do this so as to capture their experiences, achievements, interests, hopes and aspirations.

Where do I keep the All About Me book?

Talk with the child or young person about where they want to keep the book. It's their book and it's important to keep it in a safe place where it will be cared for. Keeping a soft copy of the All About Me book in case it is lost, destroyed or unreadable is highly recommended.

It is important to have a conversation with the child or young person and revisit the conversation as needed. If the child is younger and unable to express their views, you might want to add information to it to help keep their history together. The important thing is to keep adding information to it over time, so that it has the information as and when the individual asks for it.

You might want to add such information as a copy of the child or young person's birth certificate, records from their health book, which in the UK is red and in other countries blue, or black or green. This book records the development of the baby from birth to five years old, and is invaluable as a record of the child's journey of health. It may be helpful to add photographs of special events with family members, or celebrating cultural or other significant events.

What is the importance of culture?

Part of understanding your identity and helping shape a sense of belonging may be learning about and understanding your family's cultural heritage, history and family traditions.

This information helps children grow up strong and proud, knowing their parents' history and circumstances, and how they connect to communities. All About Me is a way of keeping connected to family, community and culture, and will help the child or young person develop their sense of culture and/or spirituality. It is important to provide opportunities to develop and maintain a sense of belonging to their culture/s, language/s and faith. You may be able to assist the individual with information and experiences about their cultural heritage through special events, activities like cooking and music, and participating in community traditions.

49

More About Me Books

I am often asked what More About Me work is in connection with the concept of therapeutic life story work. Questions like, what is the difference? Is it not just their therapeutic life story work, but quicker? To understand More About Me, you must first understand the reasons for doing the work, so that when you experience it, the outcome of the work and the best interests of the person you're working with is evident.

Not all children would benefit from therapeutic life story work, this being a nine-month approach, which, as a model of practice, is extremely intensive and takes the child on a journey from their grandparents all the way through to the present day and to the future.

In my model, therapeutic life story work is a very well thought-out and well-rehearsed approach to working with extremely hurt and often dissociated children and young people, where their reality is confused with the trauma, loss and often separation from their birth families – especially when that trauma has not been resolved.

Often therapeutic life story work is provided if a child or young person feels that they are defined by their past, and that past being so challenging develops further challenges to survive – it is at this stage that we need to try to support them in rediscovering their past to understand what's occurred, their role in that story, and to make sense of other roles played by the people who have been part of their life history.

By doing this, we can support children and young people to make sense of their journey and provide an opportunity to release themselves from the shame, guilt and often blame that is so unfairly felt by them. If we do our job properly, our young people will be able to move forward in a much more positive light.

We see this in relationships they began to forge, the renegotiation and resetting of relationships already experienced, and the reality that they are not only worthy, lovable and have esteem, but they can also begin to rely on other adults and people around them in the belief that they will keep them safe and they will not harm them.

Ultimately therapeutic life story work is designed to free the child or young person from the past, to understand their present and to move forward into the future, which, through support from the adults around them, they can design, shape and embrace all that is around them.

More About Me is an approach that uses a lot of the skills found within therapeutic life story work but concentrates on the particular area of need. More About Me delivered by a professionally trained therapeutic life story worker can take between 8 and 12 sessions. Each of the sessions is designed to support the child or the young person and a carer (supportive adult) to explore their journey that has led them to the particular challenge they currently face. Typically, a More About Me engagement would suit a young person who finds themself in a connected care environment, such as a Special Guardianship Order, an extended family member or a foster placement that has been given delegation of authority for them.

When children are placed in these households, it is often the case that those placed and those offering care do not have a clear understanding of how they came to be placed. They may not know the reasons for not being able to stay with their birth parents, they may not know if their birth parents are still mindful of them, they may not know if they have been left temporarily or permanently. As we all know, children and young people will blame themselves when they don't understand an event or an action. Unaddressed, this initial blame can become overwhelming for the child or young person, and they may feel it hard to invest in a connected placement, or feel that they are not good enough to be part of the new placement.

When it comes to young people placed in Special Guardianship Orders, it is often the case that they do not know what there is ahead, and so there is no clarity of the future. There may well be thoughts about the family of origin who are no longer visible, such as parents, sisters, brothers, and so forth, who may not be living together. Questions such as 'Why did I move?' 'How come I live here?' 'How long is it going to last?' 'What if it goes wrong; where will I go then?' 'Why would somebody want me to live with them if I'm so horrible that the other people I used to live with don't want me any more?'

We are not always able to explain or know what to say when difficult decisions are made in their best interests, or indeed, what does 'best interests' mean? For some children, they take on the responsibility and the blame, and in a few cases the shame. These burdens may lead to things such as self-harm, aggressive behaviours, withdrawn presentations and rejection. These, left unchecked, may develop into more concerning thoughts and emotions, and sadly stresses and anger can become aggression and internal and external harm.

To counter this, and to provide a response to support children and their carers to address their children and young people's hurts and sadness as well as other related behaviours, I brought in the notion of the More About Me book. I am so pleased that Blue Cabin has incorporated More About Me into the Creative Life Story programme.

The process is broken down into three parts; each part is essentially linked to each other so that we have an opportunity for all those involved with the child or young person, and particularly with the child or young person, to help make sense of their lives. More About Me is designed to provide children and young people (and their families) with a sense of closure from some of these past events.

The first stage is the creation of an 'Information Bank' to build a clear understanding of the child's pre-birth and post-birth history. This will develop chronologically and include evidence, both physical and written, which becomes the basis of the interaction. This approach will require the worker to collate the information, consider the validity and usefulness of the material, and then interview those involved to gain a historical perspective.

The Information Bank will not depend on the social work file, as this is only part of the story. It will include parental contributions and health information, particularly centred on the child's early years history, which will allow the worker to consider their 'internal working model' and 'attachment' issues.

Good Information Banks also provide essential information for those who are decision-makers for the child – not just social workers, but also educators, carers and health professionals. By taking time to understand where the child has come from and what part people have played in their life, the worker can begin to plan the intervention and share appropriate information with those who have care of them.

Once a clear Information Bank is created, the therapeutic life story process can move on to the second stage, called 'Internalization'. It is essential that the approach is delivered alongside the primary carer since this provides a multitude of benefits, among them the creation of a safe and contained relationship for all those involved. The development of this relationship between the carer and the child will be facilitated, promoting understanding and growth by inviting both to consider and explore through the thinking cycle already presented.

More About Me takes place over 8 to 12 sessions, and if done well, the facilitated work will support the placement and commitment between the carer and the child. The detail held within the Information Bank can be broken into session plans, and any work carried out in this fashion should be done fortnightly, each session lasting not more than an hour. The Internalization process includes 'wishes and feelings' work, exploration of feelings and the vocabulary and behavioural representation of these.

The More About Me book itself is the third stage, and this is typically presented as the evidence of the work being achieved. The book is a representation of the Internalization process explained above. That said, many children who have engaged in this process are able to decide what they have in the book as a representation for others to see, whereas the work that is completed in the direct sessions can be stored confidentially, by remaining within the second stage process.

The More About Me book concentrates on the reasons behind the current placement of the child or young person, and the decision-making and concerns that led to the life course the child or young person has experienced. It is a more concentrated therapeutic life story approach that does not present the whole life journey, but rather the sections of life history that may help to capture the child's current understanding of their world and those within it, and help the child or young person to move on.

More About Me books can also be helpful when working with children and young people who have particular challenges that can be addressed through specific incidences of historical events, such as trauma and child protection.

I am often asked by parents and carers how they might be able to help their child or young person settle, to move forward rather than living in the past, and to be safe and loved. Some carers come from similar histories and see their hurts in the hurt of the child or young person; their unresolved trauma can impact on the child's, and then we have emotionally fraught and unsafe environments. Many carers feel hopeless around the child or young person, and this hopelessness, that often turns to fear and rejection, shapes itself as a barrier to connecting with the child, especially if that child also carries a protective shield as a result of their own experienced chaos.

I have always said this, but if you want to know how to care for your child in the best way possible, then think about how you yourself would like to be cared for. This is achievable, but for some, it is too enormous a task. Our job, therefore, is to support the carer in leading, exploring, challenging, listening and learning, and through all those events and techniques, supporting the children or young person to do the same.

By listening to the stories of your young people and your children's past, we are in reach of developing a new narrative that incorporates shared lives and shared stories. In doing so, by accepting who we are, where we have been, why we are, and that, with new attachments, we are secure in the knowledge that we are going (together, rather than apart) forward, we can recover from the past.

Our stories are our anchors to the past, but these anchors are there to keep us safe and allow us to move forward when we are ready. We remove the anchors to allow this, we take risks, and we sail to the future. At times, we may need to lower our anchors to the seabed, but the seabed is different, and is now supportive. That seabed has been created by the new healthy attachments forged through More About Me.

50

Therapeutic Life Story Work

This is similar to all that has been said in the More About Me approach, but much more detailed and over three generations. The first stage in therapeutic life story work is to collate the stories of the child's grandparents, parents and older siblings, and then their story from conception to now. This will develop chronologically and include evidence, both physical and written, which becomes the basis of the interaction. This approach will require the worker to collate the information, consider the validity and usefulness of the material, and then interview those involved to gain a historical perspective.

The Information Bank will not depend on the social work file, as this is only part of the story. It will include parental contributions and health information, particularly centred on the child's early years history, which will allow the worker to consider their 'internal working model' and 'attachment' issues. The collation of physical evidence, such as pictures, first toys/books and perhaps the 'Red Book' record of development alongside the birth certificate, are helpful discussion points for the child to consider their life journey and to discuss how they might care for others in the future. It is also a positive way to demonstrate that the life story process is a journey that invites exploration and discussion.

Good Information Banks also provide essential information for those who are decision-makers for the child – not just social workers, but also educators, carers and health professionals. By taking time to understand where the child has come from and what part people have played in their life, the worker can begin to plan the intervention and share appropriate information with those who have care of them.

The model used is now referred to as the Rose Model of Therapeutic Life Story Work, and includes the three-stage process. This model requires the life story worker to understand the history and the internal working model of the child and their family. It goes on to determine the developmental level of the child, and how they may engage in the process to ensure that the right approach is used for optimum benefit. The final consideration is the environment, and whether this is conducive to the work required.

Once a clear Information Bank is created, the therapeutic life story process can move on to the second stage, called 'Internalization'. It is essential that the approach is delivered alongside the primary carer, since this provides a multitude of benefits, among them the creation of a safe and contained relationship for all those involved. The development of this relationship between the carer and the child will be facilitated, promoting understanding and growth by inviting both to consider and explore through the thinking cycle already presented.

Typically, this second stage will take about 16–18 sessions, and if done well, the facilitated work will support the placement and commitment between the carer and the child. The detail held within the Information Bank can be broken into session plans, and any work carried out in this fashion should be done fortnightly, each session lasting not more than an hour. The Internalization process includes 'wishes and feelings' work, exploration of feelings and the vocabulary and behavioural representation of these.

The Life Story book itself is the third stage, and this is typically presented as the evidence of the work being achieved. The book is a representation of the Internalization process explained above. That said, many children who have engaged in this process are able to decide what they have in the book as a representation for others to see, whereas the work that is completed in the direct sessions can be stored confidentially by remaining within the second stage process.[1]

---

[1] To find out more about the Rose Model of All About Me, More About Me and Therapeutic Life Story Work, please visit www.tlswi.com and/or purchase *The Child's Own Story*, *Life Story Therapy with Traumatised Children* (2012) and *Innovative Therapeutic Life Story Work* (2017), all published by Jessica Kingsley Publishers, London.

References

Adkin, T. and Gray-Hammond, D. (2023) 'Creating autistic suffering: What is atypical burnout?' www.emergentdivergence.com

Ainsworth, M. D. S., Blehar, M. C., Waters, E. and Wall, S. (1978) *Patterns of Attachment: A Psychological Study of the Strange Situation.* New York: Lawrence Erlbaum.

Baum, L. F. (1900) *The Wonderful Wizard of Oz.* Chicago, IL: George M. Hill Company.

Bowlby, J. (1958) 'The nature of the child's tie to his mother.' *The International Journal of Psychoanalysis 39*, 350–371.

Bowlby, J. (1988) *A Secure Base: Parent–Child Attachment and Healthy Human Development.* London: Routledge.

Brendtro, L. and Ness, A. (1983) *Re-Educating Troubled Youth: Environments for Teaching and Treatment.* New York: Walter du Gruyter.

Bronfenbrenner, U. (1977) 'Toward an experimental ecology of human development.' *American Psychologist 32*, 7, 513.

Cannon, W. B. (1929) *Bodily Changes in Pain, Hunger, Fear and Rage.* New York: D. Appleton and Company.

Carlson, J. G., Chemtob, C. M., Rusnak, K., Hedlund, N. L. and Muraoka, M. Y. (1998) 'Eye movement desensitization and reprocessing (EMDR): Treatment for combat-related post-traumatic stress disorder.' *Journal of Traumatic Stress 11*, 1, 3–24. doi: 10.1023/A:1024448814268.

Dickens, C. (1838) *Oliver Twist.* London: Richard Bentley.

Downey, L. (2007) *Calmer Classrooms: A Guide to Working with Traumatised Children. Victorian Commission for Children and Young People.* Melbourne, Victoria: Office of the Child Safety Commissioner, 9 October.

Downey, L. (2013) *Residential Care Matters: A Resource for Residential Care Workers, Supervisors and Managers Caring for Young People.* Melbourne, Victoria: Commission for Children and Young People.

Egan, G. (2002) *The Skilled Helper: A Problem-Management and Opportunity-Development Approach to Helping (7th edn).* Pacific Grove, CA: Brooks/Cole.

Gesell, A. (1929) 'Maturation and infant behavior pattern.' *Psychological Review* *36*, 4, 307–319.

Golding, K. S. (2017) *Everyday Parenting with Security and Love: Using PACE to Provide Foundations for Attachment.* London: Jessica Kingsley Publishers.

Golding, K. S. and Hughes, D. A. (2012) *Creating Loving Attachments: Parenting with PACE to Nurture Confidence and Security in the Troubled Child.* London: Jessica Kingsley Publishers.

Gottman, J. M. with DeClaire, J. (1998) *Raising an Emotionally Intelligent Child.* New York: Simon & Schuster.

Greenwald, R. (2005) *Child Trauma Handbook: A Guide for Helping Trauma-Exposed Children and Adolescents.* London: Routledge.

Greenwald, R. [art by Baden, K. J.] (2007) *A Fairy Tale* [Comic book]. Northampton, MA: Trauma Institute & Child Trauma Institute.

Gulden, H. and Vick, C. (2010) *Learning the Dance of Attachment: An Adoptive Foster Parent's Guide to Nurturing Healthy Development.* Lulu.com

Hughes, D. A. (2004) *Building the Bonds of Attachment: Awakening Love in Deeply Troubled Children.* Lanham, MD: Rowman & Littlefield.

Hughes, D. A. and Golding, K. S. (2024) *Healing Relational Trauma Workbook: Dyadic Developmental Psychotherapy in Practice.* New York: W. W. Norton & Co.

Hughes, D. A., Golding, K. S. and Hudson, J. (2019) *Healing Relational Trauma with Attachment-Focused Interventions: Dyadic Developmental Psychotherapy with Children and Families.* New York: W. W. Norton & Co.

James, B. (1989) *Treating Traumatized Children: New Insights and Creative Interventions.* New York: The Free Press.

James, B. (2008) *Handbook for Treatment of Attachment-Trauma Problems in Children.* New York: The Free Press.

King, S. (1997) *Wizard and Glass: The Dark Tower IV.* London: Hodder & Stoughton.

Kipling, R. (1902) 'The Elephant's Child.' In *Just So Stories.* London: Macmillan.

Klein, M. (1920) 'The Development of a Child.' In *The Writings of Melanie Klein, vol. I* (pp.1–53). London: Hogarth.

Klein, M. (1952) *Notes on Some Schizoid Mechanisms 1: Developments in Psychoanalysis.* Abingdon: Routledge.

Levy, T. M. and Orlans, M. (2014) *Attachment, Trauma and Healing: Understanding and Treating Attachment Disorder in Children, Families and Adults.* London: Jessica Kingsley Publishers.

MacLean, P. D. (ed.) (1990) *The Triune Brain in Evolution: Role in Paleo Cerebral Functions.* New York: Plenum Press.

Maslow, A. H. (1943) 'A theory of human motivation.' *Psychological Review* *50*, 370–396.

Maslow, A. H. (1987) *Motivation and Personality (3rd edn).* Delhi, India: Pearson Education.

Oaklander, V. (2015) *Windows to Our Children (2nd edn).* Gouldsboro, ME: The Gestalt Journal Press.

Perls, F. (1973) The *Gestalt Approach and Eye Witness to Therapy*. Palo Alto, CA: Science and Behavior Books.

Perry, B. D. and Szalavitz, M. (2007) *The Boy Who Was Raised as a Dog: And Other Stories from a Child Psychiatrist's Notebook. What Traumatized Children Can Teach Us About Loss, Love and Healing.* New York: Basic Books.

Perry, B. D. and Winfrey, O. (2021) *What Happened to You? Conversations on Trauma, Resilience and Healing.* New York: Flatiron Books.

Porges, S. W. (2001) 'The polyvagal theory: Phylogenetic substrates of a social nervous system.' *International Journal of Psychophysiology 42*, 2, 123–146. doi: 10.1016/s0167-8760(01)00162-3.

Purvis, K. and Quails, L. (2020) *The Connected Parent: Real-Life Strategies for Building Trust and Attachment.* Eugene, OR: Harvest House Publishers.

Rose, R. (2012) *Life Story Therapy with Traumatised Children: A Model for Practice.* London: Jessica Kingsley Publishers.

Rose, R. (2017) *Innovative Therapeutic Life Story Work.* London: Jessica Kingsley Publishers.

Rose, R. and Philpot, T. (2004) *The Child's Own Story: Life Story Work with Traumatized Children.* London: Jessica Kingsley Publishers.

Rowling, J. K. (1993) *Harry Potter and the Prisoner of Azkaban.* London: Bloomsbury.

Schore, A. (2000) 'Attachment and the regulation of the right brain.' *Attachment & Human Development 2*, 1, 23–47. doi: 10.1080/146167300361309.

Shapiro, F. (1989) 'Efficacy of the eye movement desensitization procedure in the treatment of traumatic memories.' *Journal of Traumatic Stress 2*, 2, 199–223. https://doi.org/10.1002/jts.2490020207

Stansbury, K. and Harris, M. L. (2000) 'Individual differences in stress reactions during a peer entry episode: Effects of age, temperament, approach behavior, and self-perceived peer competence.' *Science Journal of Experimental Child Psychology 76*, 1, 50–63. https://doi.org/10.1006/jecp.1999.2541

Stern, D. (1983) 'Affect Attunement.' In J. D. Call, E. Galenson and R. L. Tyson (eds) *Frontiers of Infant Psychiatry* (pp.33–44). New York: Harper & Row.

Thomas, L. (2019) 'What is trauma?' Australian Childhood Foundation Blog, 5 March. https://professionals.childhood.org.au/prosody/2019/03/what-is-trauma

Turnell, A. and Edwards, S. (1999) *Signs of Safety: A Solution and Safety Oriented Approach to Child Protection Casework.* New York: W. W. Norton & Co.

van der Kolk, B. (1998) 'Trauma and memory.' *Psychiatry and Clinical Neurosciences 52*, S1, S1–S108. https://doi.org/10.1046/j.1440-1819.1998.0520s5S97.x

van der Kolk, B. (2015) *The Body Keeps the Score: Brain, Mind, and Body in the Healing of Trauma.* London: Penguin Books.

Walker, P. (2013) *Complex PTSD: From Surviving to Thriving.* Lafayette, CA: Azure Coyote Publishing.

Webb, R. (2017) *How Not to Be a Boy.* London: Canongate.

Winnicott, D. W. (1945) 'Primitive emotional development.' *The International Journal of Psychoanalysis 26*, 137–143.

Winnicott, D. W. (1960) 'The Theory of the Parent-Infant Relationship.' In D. W. Winnicott (1965) *The Maturational Processes and the Facilitating Environment* (pp.37–55). New York: International Universities Press.

Further reading

Ainsworth, M. D. (1964) 'Patterns of attachment behavior shown by the infant in interaction with his mother.' *Merrill-Palmer Quarterly of Behavior and Development 10*, 1, 51–58. www.jstor.org/stable/23082925

Ainsworth, M. D. (1979) 'Attachment as related to mother–infant interaction.' *Advances in the Study of Behavior 9*, 1–51. https://doi.org/10.1016/S0065-3454(08)60032-7

Ainsworth, M. D. S. and Bell, S. M. (1970) 'Attachment, exploration, and separation: Illustrated by the behavior of one-year-olds in a strange situation.' *Child Development 41*, 1, 49–67. https://doi.org/10.2307/1127388

Perry, B. (2006) 'The Neurosequential Model of Therapeutics: Applying Principles of Neuroscience to Clinical Work with Traumatized and Maltreated Children.' In N. Boyd Webb (ed.) *Working with Traumatized Youth in Child Welfare* (pp.27–52). New York: Guilford Press.

Perry, B. D. and Dobson, C. (2009) 'Surviving childhood trauma: The role of relationships in prevention of, and recovery from, trauma-related problems.' *Journal of CCYP, a division of British Association for Counselling and Psychotherapy*, March, 28–31.

Siegel, D. J. (2014) *Brainstorm: The Power and Purpose of the Teenage Brain*. London: Scribe UK.